The Educator's Guide to

PREVENTING AND SOLVING DISCIPLINE PROBLEMS

MARK BOYNTON & CHRISTINE BOYNTON

ASSOCIATION FOR SUPERVISION AND CURRICULUM DEVELOPMENT
ALEXANDRIA, VIRGINIA USA

Association for Supervision and Curriculum Development
1703 N. Beauregard St. • Alexandria, VA 22311-1714 USA
Phone: 800-933-2723 or 703-578-9600 • Fax: 703-575-5400
Web site: www.ascd.org • E-mail: member@ascd.org
Author guidelines: www.ascd.org/write

Gene R. Carter, *Executive Director;* Nancy Modrak, *Director of Publishing;* Julie Houtz, *Director of Book Editing & Production;* Ernesto Yermoli, *Project Manager;* Georgia Park, *Senior Graphic Designer;* Keith Demmons, *Desktop Publishing Specialist;* Vivian Coss, *Production Specialist*

ASCD Member Book, No. FY06-02 (November 2005, PC). ASCD Member Books mail to Premium (P), Comprehensive (C), and Regular (R) members on this schedule: Jan., PC; Feb., P; Apr., PCR; May, P; July, PC; Aug., P; Sept., PCR; Nov., PC; Dec., P.

Paperback ISBN: 1-4166-0237-2 • ASCD product #105124
e-books: retail PDF ISBN 1-4166-0326-3 • netLibrary ISBN 1-4166-0324-7 • ebrary ISBN 1-4166-0325-5

Quantity discounts for the paperback book: 10–49 copies, 10%; 50+ copies, 15%; for 500 or more copies, call 800-933-2723, ext. 5634, or 703-575-5634.

Library of Congress Cataloging-in-Publication Data
Boynton, Mark, 1947-
  The educator's guide to preventing and solving discipline problems / Mark Boynton & Christine Boynton.
     p. cm.
  Includes bibliographical references and index.
  ISBN 1-4166-0237-2 (alk. paper)
  1. School discipline--United States. 2. Classroom management--United States. I. Boynton, Christine, 1947- II. Title.
  LB3011.B63 2005
  371.102'4--dc22
                              2005024033

10 09 08 07 06 05   12 11 10 9 8 7 6 5 4 3 2 1

The Educator's Guide to
PREVENTING AND SOLVING
DISCIPLINE PROBLEMS

Introduction

This book is about developing effective classroom and buildingwide discipline systems. It is based on the belief that the most effective discipline systems use proactive strategies designed to prevent discipline problems rather than strategies intended to correct problems after they occur. Because we know that prevention does not always work, the book also includes strategies to use when prevention approaches are not enough.

This book is also based on the belief that the one factor that affects staff morale, job satisfaction, and building climate more than any other is classroom and buildingwide discipline. According to Zehm and Kottler (1993), discipline problems are teachers' number-one complaint about their jobs. Marzano (2003) says that the public judges the effectiveness of a school by its management of student behavior. Nothing affects a building's reputation more than the level of discipline that permeates the classrooms and overall school. No staff member wants to work in a classroom or building that is chaotic or out of control. Excellent teachers request transfers from these buildings, and parents attempt to move their students out of these schools. Soon there is a vicious cycle of staff exodus, parental complaints, and declining test scores.

Whether staff believe they control student behaviors or not, they are right! Most students will behave appropriately when each and every staff member holds expectations for appropriate behaviors, when effective discipline systems are in place, when these systems are taught to students, and when students are held accountable for their actions.

Creating and maintaining effective levels of classroom and buildingwide discipline is hard work. There are certain approaches and components to student discipline that staff members must understand, accept, and embrace if they are to attain this critical goal. They must embrace the belief that developing positive relationships with students is an essential step toward establishing a structured and orderly classroom and building environment, as students will work to please adults whose actions make it clear that they respect and care for the students. Realizing that students learn what is taught and not what is announced, teachers must formally teach their discipline expectations just as they teach any content area of the curriculum. It is also imperative that teachers have a variety of immediate, meaningful, varied, and easy-to-implement consequences for students who fail to comply with the discipline policies and procedures. Finally, administrators and parents need to support teachers as they hold students accountable for their behaviors.

The goal of this book is to clearly articulate classroom and building-wide discipline strategies that every teacher and every building can use today. It begins with components of classroom discipline and offers universal techniques for teachers. It then moves to buildingwide philosophies and methods of discipline.

The strategies in this book apply to all students, but they focus on what we call the "fence-rider kids." Fence-rider kids, who make up 15 percent of all students, are the students whose behaviors are dramatically influenced by the discipline policies used in a classroom or a building. Curwin and Mendler (1988) refer to the 80-15-5 principle that exists in classrooms: 80 percent of the students consistently follow the rules, 15 percent occasionally break the rules, and 5 percent often break the rules. The 15 percent who occasionally break the rules are the fence-rider kids, and they can be our best-behaved or our worst-behaved students. They are the students who will behave perfectly in one classroom environment and then become disruptors in another, depending on the teacher's style and expectations. Their behaviors are malleable, reflecting the actions and reactions of their teachers. Our goal is to expand the repertoire of positive actions that teachers can take to influence these students' behaviors and consequently make a positive difference in their classroom environment.

Even though the concepts reviewed in this book apply to all students at all levels, we recognize that there are developmental differences among students at elementary, middle, and high school levels. Staff members must consider these differences as they reflect on how best to apply the principles and strategies to their specific situations and grade levels.

In the last section of the book are strategies for particularly difficult students, such as bullies and those with anger management issues, oppositional defiant disorder (ODD), or attention deficit hyperactivity disorder (ADHD). These are the 5 percent of the students that Curwin and Mendler (1988) refer to in their 80-15-5 principle. This group of students requires strategies and plans above and beyond what we normally use with the fence-rider kids. Although the techniques in the final section are recommended for students who have been identified as difficult, they can be effectively used with all students. This last section also discusses ways to respond to classroom disruptions and how to deal with major rule violations.

At the end of each section are reflection questions reinforcing major concepts. These questions can be used for individual study or as points of discussion with staff who are meeting to review and revise their discipline systems.

CRUCIAL COMPONENTS OF EFFECTIVE CLASSROOM DISCIPLINE

Crucial Components of Effective Classroom Discipline

How does a teacher, especially a brand-new classroom teacher, establish an atmosphere that's exciting and stimulating, but at the same time has effective levels of classroom discipline? Good student management is vitally important for every teacher. Not only will it create a positive climate; it also will dramatically affect student learning.

In a study reviewing 11,000 pieces of research that spanned 50 years, Wang, Haertel, and Walberg (1993/1994) identified 28 factors that influence student learning. The most important one was classroom management.

The good news is that teachers can learn to become better classroom managers. We believe there are four components that, when implemented correctly, are crucial for establishing an effective classroom discipline system: positive teacher-student relations, clearly defined parameters of acceptable student behaviors, monitoring skills, and consequences. (A critical fifth component of effective discipline, which is beyond the scope of this book, is good, strong content instruction.) We have developed a diagram illustrating what we believe is the ideal relationship among these four components of classroom discipline. The percentages in this diagram are based on the model developed by French and Raven (1960), in which they identified the five bases of social power teachers use to influence students: referent power, coercive power, legitimate power, expert power, and reward power.

Referent power, probably the most influential, is based on the strong relationship of caring the student has for the teacher. Coercive power is the power students perceive teachers to have because of their ability to give punishments. Legitimate power flows from the teacher's position of authority over the students. Expert power is the power a teacher has because of his or her special knowledge regarding the curriculum content and disciplinary strategies. Reward power is the power students perceive teachers to have because they can withhold or give them rewards for their behaviors (Tauber, 1999).

French and Raven (1960) state that these five bases are used by educators to wield power over students, just as they are used in other social relationships. Tauber (1999) claims that, depending on their own personal belief systems, teachers adjust the power bases they use in their interactions with students. He gives an example of one situation in which a teacher's belief system and practice results in the use of 20 percent expert power, 55 percent referent power, 15 percent legitimate power, 5 percent reward power, and 5 percent coercive power. In a second example, another teacher uses 5 percent expert power, 5 percent referent power, 10 percent legitimate power, 45 percent reward power, and 35 percent coercive power.

In our model, based on our belief in the importance of relationships with students, we call for 40 percent referent power (relationships), followed by 25 percent legitimate power (clear parameters of acceptable behaviors), 25 percent expert power (monitoring skills), and, finally, 10 percent reward and coercive power together (consequences). Figure S1 illustrates what we believe is the ideal relationship among these power bases and what we term the four crucial components of classroom discipline.

FIGURE S1

THE FOUR CRUCIAL DISCIPLINE COMPONENTS

Consequences 10%

Positive teacher-student relationships 40%

Clear parameters of acceptable behaviors 25%

Monitoring skills 25%

The trick is to build a classroom discipline system around the first three components—positive teacher-student relationships, clear parameters, and monitoring skills—and to artfully and naturally integrate them into your classroom instruction so that they are just part of the way you do business and interact with students. When they are implemented effectively, it will be difficult for an untrained observer to separate them from your classroom instruction. Even more important, they become a powerful preventive approach to classroom discipline that greatly diminishes the need to use consequences or punishments.

The fourth component is the use of negative consequences for misbehavior. Even the most skilled teacher needs to include clearly defined and articulated consequences within his or her discipline plan. Although necessary, consequences should be the least-used component of the plan.

The chapters in this section focus on specific strategies for developing each of the four components of effective discipline: positive teacher-student relationships, clearly defined parameters of acceptable student behaviors, monitoring skills, and consequences.

1

Developing Positive
Teacher-Student Relations

We all want to feel cared for and valued by the significant people in our world. Students are no different. This knowledge is a powerful tool in the arsenal available to you as you form your classroom discipline plan. As a classroom teacher, you wield a great deal of power over your students simply due to the fact that you control their destiny for up to six and a half hours each day, five days a week. When students feel that you value and care for them as individuals, they are more willing to comply with your wishes.

Think about it for just a minute. Aren't you more apt to go out of your way to please a boss who you feel values you as an individual and treats you with dignity and respect, rather than a boss who communicates a lack of respect for you? When your boss asks about your family, gives you "slack" when there is a personal emergency, or praises you for work well done, don't you develop feelings of regard for this boss and want to do your best to please him or her? Students have the same feelings. So it makes sense that developing positive teacher-student relations is one of the most effective steps you can take to establish a positive discipline climate in the classroom. It's critical to remember that when you treat students with respect, they tend to appreciate and like you. When they appreciate and like you, they are more willing to want to please you—which causes them to be more likely to behave appropriately. This is why it is so important to remember that, when it comes to student behavior, it's far more often the relationship students have with you than it is the rules themselves that encourages students to follow those rules.

A review of the research shows that authors have a lot to say about positive relationships with students. Thompson (1998) says, "The most powerful weapon available to secondary teachers who want to foster a favorable learning climate is a positive relationship with our students" (p. 6). Canter and Canter (1997) make the statement that we all can recall classes in which we did not try very hard because we didn't like our teachers. This should remind us how important it is to have strong, positive relationships with our students. Kohn (1996) goes a step further, saying, "Children are more likely to be respectful when important adults in their lives respect them. They are more likely to care about others if they know they are cared about" (p. 111). Marzano (2003) states that students will resist rules and procedures along with the consequent disciplinary actions if the foundation of a good relationship is lacking. He goes on to assert that relationships are perhaps more important at the elementary and junior high levels than at the high school level. And according to Zehm and Kottler (1993), students will never trust us or open themselves up to hear what we have to say unless they sense that we value and respect them.

As we showed in Figure S1, strategies to develop positive teacher-student relations should be the largest portion of your discipline plan. What are some strategies that you can implement to develop strong and powerful relationships with your students? Let's look at some techniques that are easy to integrate into your everyday interactions with students: communicating positive expectations, correcting students in a constructive way, developing positive classroom pride, demonstrating caring, and preventing and reducing your own frustration and stress.

Communicating Positive Expectations

Research on teacher expectations and student achievement has shown that expectations have a dramatic impact on student academic performance (Kerman, Kimball, & Martin, 1980). Student behavioral performance is also dependent to a large degree on the expectations of significant adults in students' lives. Numerous studies indicate that the expectations teachers have for students tend to become self-fulfilling prophesies. It is therefore critically important for educators to monitor their interactions with the goal of communicating appropriately high behavioral and academic expectations to all students, not just to high achievers.

There are several techniques that can be used to achieve this goal. Monitor the way you call on students. Make sure that you give all students chances to participate in class. Try to increase the amount of time you wait between asking a student a question and moving on by either answering the question yourself or calling on another student. Give students hints and clues to help them succeed in class. Tell students directly that you believe that they have the ability to do well. Your belief in them will inspire their success.

Let's look at some of these techniques for communicating high expectations in more detail and discuss ways to implement these techniques in your classroom.

Call on All Students Equitably

When you call on students, there are several things to keep in mind. First of all, you must monitor the equitability of response opportunities. Often, teachers who keep track discover that they call on a small number of students frequently and allow few, if any, chances for students for whom they have low expectations to answer. When you fail to recognize particular students, you can communicate a low level of confidence in their abilities. Individual students may "tune out" and believe that you don't expect they will be able to answer your questions. This message is compounded when these students see others being called on regularly.

Think about what it would communicate to you if your boss always asked other teachers to participate in committee work or special projects instead of you. And how would you feel if the boss continually came to you for help on curriculum projects or input on difficult students? Just as we do, students develop feelings of self-confidence in their abilities when their teacher goes to them for the right answer. In addition, calling on all the students in your class—rather than a select few—will help keep students on task and decrease the number of behavior problems.

It is important that you monitor yourself to be certain that you are providing all of your students with response opportunities. Putting a check by the name of each student you call on during class discussions is an excellent way to quickly determine whether you are being equitable. Also, you should monitor yourself to make certain you are not calling exclusively on your high-achieving students but also on students who have a pattern of not performing well.

Keeping a simple checklist on a clipboard during classroom discussions is a great strategy you can easily implement. Figure 1.1 is an example of such a checklist. In this example, you can see that Donna and Sam are getting the majority of the response opportunities. This could be because the teacher has confidence in these students, knows that calling on them will keep the discussion moving, and wants the other students to hear the correct answers. However, it also could lead the other students to think that the teacher doesn't have confidence in them and doesn't expect them to participate, and it increases the likelihood that they will get off task. If you were the teacher, you would want to be sure that before the end of the discussion you called on all your students so as to make the discussion more equitable.

FIGURE 1.1

SAMPLE CHECKLIST FOR MONITORING EQUITABLE
RESPONSE OPPORTUNITIES

Paul Brown: ✓ ✓
Charlie Cash: ✓
Donna Dawson: ✓ ✓ ✓
Frank Freeze: ✓
Mary Jones:
Sam Smith: ✓ ✓ ✓

Try to make an effort to call on students who have typically been off task or who have been achieving at a low level, allowing them to respond and participate in class, and watch what happens. Over time, you will notice that these students will remain on task more often and improve academically! This change does not occur immediately, but it definitely does occur and is extremely gratifying to see.

Increase Latency Periods When Questioning Students

Increasing latency (Kerman et al., 1980) is another technique you can use to communicate that you have positive expectations for a student. Latency is the amount of time that elapses between the moment you give a student a response opportunity and the moment you terminate the response opportunity. Kerman and colleagues (1980) explain that the amount of time we give to students to answer questions is directly related to the level of expectation we have for them. We give more time to students when we have confidence in their ability to answer a question. Conversely, we give less time to students in whom we have little confidence. When you quickly give up on a student who is struggling with a response, it is clear to everyone in the classroom that you don't expect him or her to come up with the right answer. In addition, when you give up on a student who initially struggles with a response, the student realizes that all he or she needs to do to "get off the hook" is respond to your question with a confused expression or blank stare. What you will find when you make a conscious effort to extend the length of latency you allow for low-achieving students is that these students will begin to pay more attention, become more actively involved in discussions, and minimize their behavior issues. One thing you can do is ask a teaching peer to observe your instruction and chart the length of the latency periods you are giving each student from the time you ask the question until you move on to another student. It is especially interesting to find out which students get longer latency periods from you. Figure 1.2 shows an example of a latency chart.

FIGURE 1.2

LATENCY CHART IN SECONDS

Paul Brown: 1, 3

Charlie Cash:

Donna Dawson: 5, 6, 8

Frank Freeze: 1, 1

Mary Jones: 8, 10, 8

Sam Smith:

In analyzing the chart, it is easy to see that Donna and Mary are consistently given more latency and, therefore, more chances to give a correct response than are the other students. If this were your classroom, you could try to make sure that in future discussions and question-and-answer periods you give longer latency periods to other students as well before moving on.

Give Hints and Clues to Help Students Answer Questions

You also communicate positive expectations by giving hints and clues to your students. In their work on teacher expectations, Kerman and colleagues (1980) point out that teachers usually do more "delving and rephrasing" for students for whom they have high expectations and less for students for whom they have low expectations. It is important that we communicate to all our students that we have high expectations for their success, and one way to do this is by giving more hints and clues to all students, especially the low-performing students.

Think about a reading lesson in which a student struggles to sound out a word. After waiting for an appropriate latency period, the teacher might prompt, "It sounds like 'cat.'" In a secondary classroom, a teacher could ask, "What were the three causes of the War of 1812?" After the latency period, the teacher might say, "Think about what we learned regarding the British treatment of U.S. sailors."

There are things to be cautious about when using this technique. If you provide too many hints and clues, you may actually give the student the answer. Also, after a number of hints, it may be that the only student who doesn't know the answer is the one being called on, which ends up being an embarrassing experience. The important point, however, is to use hints and clues with all students to communicate that you have high expectations for the entire class. This helps build positive teacher-student relations.

Tell Students They Have the Ability to Do Well

Another way to communicate positive expectations to students is by directly telling them they have the ability to do well. When you tell your students you have confidence that they can handle a difficult assignment or improve their behavior, you impart a very powerful message. Students often will work hard and behave appropriately to prove that your confidence in them is justified. Every child needs to have at least one significant adult in his or her life who believes that he or she can do well. Ideally, children would hear this from their parents, but the sad truth is that is not always the case. Teachers have the unique opportunity and privilege to communicate daily to a number of students that they believe in them.

What a gift to be able to be that significant adult in even one student's life.

Using this strategy might lead a teacher to say this to a student: "Emma, I know you'll do your best on this math test. You've been working very hard on remembering to write down your thinking as you solve math problems, and I know you can transfer that skill to this test. I'll check back with you later." This approach can be modified for any grade level or subject area. Once again, this is a positive relations strategy as well as an instructional strategy.

You can also let students know that you have positive expectations for them by referring to past successes (Kerman et al., 1980). When you tell a student that you know he will behave appropriately at recess because he was successful yesterday, you help build confidence in the student and increase his chance for success. And after a student demonstrates good behavior or academic achievement in a specific situation, telling her you knew she would be successful (Kerman et al., 1980) also instills confidence and a culture of positive expectations. Students need to know that their teachers respect them and have confidence in them. Using these different strategies to consistently communicate your positive expectations will work wonders. We challenge you to begin using one or two of these strategies today to build high expectations and positive teacher-student relations.

Correcting Students in a Constructive Way

Correcting and disciplining students for inappropriate behaviors is a necessary and important part of every teacher's job. However, it doesn't have to be a negative part of your job. In fact, you can actually build positive relationships when you correct students. If you don't believe this, think for just a minute about students you have had in the past who came back to school to visit you. Often it is the students who were the most challenging and with whom you had to spend the most time who continue to visit you over the years. This is due to the positive relationships you developed with them.

The goal in correcting students should be to have them reflect on what they did, be sorry that they disappointed you, and make a better choice in the future. It should not be that they go away thinking, "I hate my teacher. I'm going to be sure I don't get caught next time." The difference in students' reactions to being disciplined is often related to the manner in which you correct them. If you allow students to keep their dignity, you increase the chance that they will reflect on their behavior and choose their behaviors more wisely in the future. The correction process will be counterproductive if students are corrected in a manner that communicates bitterness, sarcasm, low expectations, or disgust. The goal is to provide a quick, fair, and meaningful consequence while at the same time communicating that you care for and respect the student.

Figure 1.3 outlines steps to be taken when correcting or disciplining a student.

FIGURE 1.3

STEPS TO USE WHEN CORRECTING STUDENTS

1. Review what happened
2. Identify and accept the student's feelings
3. Review alternative actions
4. Explain the building policy as it applies to the situation
5. Let the student know that all students are treated the same
6. Invoke an immediate and meaningful consequence
7. Let the student know you are disappointed that you have to invoke a consequence to his or her action
8. Communicate an expectation that the student will do better in the future

---

Imagine that Johnny hit Sam because Sam called his mother a name. This is how you could put these disciplinary steps in place:

1. *Review what happened.* Discuss the incident with Johnny. Begin with fact finding to be sure that you are appropriately correcting the student. The worst way to affect teacher-student relationships is to unfairly discipline a student.

2. *Identify and accept the student's feelings.* Tell Johnny that you understand why it upset him to hear somebody call his mother a name and that you, too, would be upset if someone maligned your mother. It's important to understand that this step communicates that you respect and understand his feelings but that you are not accepting his actions.

3. *Review alternative actions.* Go over with Johnny the different actions he could have taken, such as ignoring the remark or reporting it to a teacher.

4. *Explain the building policy as it applies to the situation.* Remind Johnny of the building policy of not fighting and that the rule is if anyone hits another student, he or she will be sent to the office and possibly be suspended from school.

5. *Let the student know that all students are treated the same.* Make sure that Johnny understands that all students must adhere to the policy and that any student who disregards the rule will suffer the consequences.

6. *Invoke an immediate and meaningful consequence.* Communicate with the office about what happened and send Johnny to the office.

7. *Let the student know you are disappointed that you have to invoke a consequence to his or her action.* Tell Johnny that you are disappointed that his actions have led to this situation.

8. *Communicate an expectation that the student will do better in the future.* Remind Johnny that, although you do not approve of his actions and do not like to send him or any student to the office, you like him and know that he will make a better choice next time. Also tell him that you are there to support him and work through these issues with him in the future.

In addition to your following these steps when correcting a student, it is important to keep some key philosophical precepts in mind. First of all, remember to correct the student in a private location. Although it is not always possible to remove a student from the classroom, do your best to prevent visual access by other students as you discipline. Public correction can foster feelings of anger, embarrassment, and bitterness; it can also become a sideshow for the other students. Also, when invoking a consequence, you should ask yourself, "How would I want my own children disciplined in a similar situation?" Answering this question will help you treat the student with care and respect. Finally, remember to stay calm and avoid frustration. The worst thing you can do is to invoke a consequence when you are angry or upset, as this can lead to regrettable actions on your part. If necessary, give yourself a "cooling-off period" before intervening with the student. Figure 1.4 reviews the key philosophical considerations for correcting students.

FIGURE 1.4

KEY PHILOSOPHICAL PRECEPTS WHEN CORRECTING STUDENTS

- Correct in a private location
- Treat students as you want your own children treated
- Stay calm
- Avoid frustration

It is also important to follow certain steps after disciplining a student. These steps are shown in Figure 1.5.

FIGURE 1.5

STEPS TO FOLLOW AFTER DISCIPLINING A STUDENT

1. Touch base with the student
2. Acknowledge postdisciplinary successes
3. Don't give up too quickly

Let's go back to the example of Johnny, in which he earned an office referral because he hit Sam. Here are some actions you could take:

1. *Touch base with the student.* Follow up with Johnny after the consequence, checking to see how he's doing and simply making contact with him.

2. *Acknowledge postdisciplinary successes.* The next time Johnny has difficulty with a student and handles the situation more appropriately, such as by verbalizing his displeasure rather than using his fists, be sure to acknowledge his behavior and praise him for making the right choice.

3. *Don't give up too quickly.* Finally, don't forget that some students respond negatively to positive attention. In such cases, it may appear that the student doesn't want the positive attention. What may actually be happening is a gradual change in the student's self-concept.

> **Tip Box**
>
> *Remember:* Students will recall how you made them feel long after they have forgotten the consequence they earned as a result of their actions.

When students are used to getting into trouble and having negative attention, it takes a while to break this cycle. Often it is just a matter of time before the student starts to show the positive effects of this attention, so don't give up!

Developing Positive Classroom Pride

If applied effectively, pride can be an extremely powerful force in developing positive teacher-student relationships (Kerman et al., 1980). In many classrooms, students are proud of the fact that they are behaving and achieving at a high level. In other classrooms, a different type of pride develops when students see themselves as being the worst they can be. The pride students develop helps shape identities that in turn drive their behaviors. When you recognize student successes, there is a decreased likelihood of fostering negative pride and an increased likelihood of developing positive pride. As a classroom teacher, your goal should be to help students take pride in their accomplishments and positive behaviors rather than in their negative behaviors. Figure 1.6 lists some strategies that will help you attain this important goal.

FIGURE 1.6

STRATEGIES TO DEVELOP POSITIVE CLASSROOM PRIDE

- Display student work
- Positively reinforce students verbally
- Show off the class's achievements
- Speak to the accomplishments of all your students
- Be sincere in your pride in your students
- Look for opportunities for students to be proud in all areas
- Develop parental pride in student accomplishments
- Develop pride in improvement in addition to pride in excellence

---

Displaying student work is a good way to let students know that you value the work they do and that you take pride in their work products. The displayed work does not have to be perfect and should show a significant cross section of the students you have in your class. Putting the work of students who have a history of low achievement up on a bulletin board often helps to build their self-esteem and pride and encourages them to do better work in the future. Exhibiting the work throughout the building in hallways, in the office, and in other public areas can do a great deal to develop positive levels of student pride. The impact becomes even more powerful when you let the class know that you want others to see the great work they are doing. An example of this would be to display all your students' science projects in the library and telling your class, "You all did a great job on your science projects, including stating your problem and hypothesis, clearly writing out the steps you took, and then drawing conclusions. I am so proud of all of you that I wanted the whole school to see your exemplary work. That's why I put all the projects on display in the library."

Positively reinforce students verbally on a regular basis. Tell your students when you are pleased by their behavior. Let them know that you're not surprised when they grasp a difficult concept. This is a powerful way of developing positive pride.

Publicly asking other staff members to enter the classroom so that they can see a specific accomplishment of your class, such as the way they respond to your instructions, is an example of *showing off the class's achievements.* However, be careful to *speak to the accomplishments of all the students* when you use this strategy rather than to the accomplishments of just the top students, or the strategy could backfire on you.

There are numerous opportunities to *develop pride in all areas,* such as by publicly recognizing high test scores, acts of kindness, positive citizenship, and athletic accomplishments. You can also extend the pride taken in the class by *developing parental pride in student accomplishments.* Provide opportunities for parents to review student work in newsletters, during back-to-school events, and at parent conferences. Let parents know about high attendance rates, high test scores, and the percentage of homework or assignments completed. In this way, you are enlisting parents to be your partners in fostering this powerful positive relationship tool.

Remember that pride does not always have to involve only excellence. *Pride in improvement* is an important type of pride to nurture. Test scores and daily assignments that go from a *D* to a *C* and homework that starts coming in on time are examples of great opportunities for you to recognize student success and build pride.

When Kelley, a new teacher, took over a 6th grade class at a large elementary school in January, he used a combination of these approaches to build pride in the students. The class had already "gotten rid of" two other teachers, and they were proud of being the "baddest" class in the school. Besides teaching clearly defined parameters for appropriate behaviors and strong consequences for negative behaviors, Kelley gradually worked at building positive pride with the class. While practicing walking in the hallways and transitioning between activities appropriately with the class, he would invite the principal or other teachers in and say, "I just wanted you to see what a great job my class is doing and how proud I am of the respectful and quiet way they are walking in the halls." After working with the students on how he wanted them to respond when he gave his signal, he would again invite other staff into the room and say, "Look at how quickly and quietly my class responds to my signal. They have really improved. Aren't they great?" In addition, he would tell the students on a regular basis that he couldn't wait to get to school each day because it was so much fun working with them and because he was so proud of their improved behaviors and academics. This continued focus on building positive classroom pride gradually changed the pride the class had in their negative behaviors to pride in their new culture of positive behaviors.

These are just some of the ways you can work to develop student pride individually and collectively. This in turn will help you build positive relationships with your students. A key element of Kelley's success was that he was sincere in his proclamations of pride in his students. Children are intuitive regarding sincerity, and insincere comments will quickly backfire.

One caution for secondary teachers concerning pride involves a distinction between the manner in which you foster pride for different grade levels of students. What works for elementary and middle school students is not necessarily appropriate at the high school level. Sprick (1985) points out that it's more effective to use calm, quiet statements with secondary students than emotional praise, as they get embarrassed and don't like to be singled out from their peers. We believe you can and should instill positive pride with secondary students, but a more private method may be more effective.

Demonstrating Caring

Demonstrating caring is one of the most powerful ways to build positive relationships with your students (Kerman et al., 1980). When your actions and words communicate that you sincerely care for your students, they are more likely to want to perform well for you and enjoy coming to school. Caring also fosters a preventive approach to discipline, as students who feel cared for are more likely to want to please you by complying with your wishes and policies. It is a tragedy when a student mistakenly believes that his teacher does not care for or like him. In most cases, teachers do care but fail to do the things that directly communicate this valuable message. Figure 1.7 lists some strategies to communicate to your students that you care about them.

FIGURE 1.7

STRATEGIES TO SHOW YOU CARE

- Show an interest in your students' personal lives
- Greet the students by the front door as they enter the classroom
- Watch for and touch base with students who display strong emotion
- Sincerely listen to students
- Empathize with students

Inquiring about aspects of students' personal lives is a powerful way to communicate that the students are important and cared for. You can do this by asking about a recent trip, a hobby, or a sports activity. Some teachers make it a point to watch sporting events that their students are involved in, which is a wonderful way to show students you care about them beyond the classroom walls. The caution with this approach is to be as equitable as possible so that there is not a perception that you have "favorites." A proactive way to do this is to have students write a journal at the beginning of the year in which they list what they did during their vacation, what pets they have, what sports they enjoy, and what hobbies they have. With this information, you can look for opportunities to ask questions or make comments to individual students using these facts. You might say to one student, "Susie, I read that you have a cocker spaniel. I have one, too. Does your dog know any tricks?"

Standing by the door and welcoming students as they enter the classroom is a quick and easy way to show students they are important and that you are glad to see them. This procedure also helps you start the day with personal contact with each and every student. This is a procedure Wong and Wong (1998) advocate as a way to begin the day and the school year on a positive note.

When you see *students display strong emotions* (e.g., when they are happy, excited, or angry), you have an opportunity to build positive relationships by asking how they are doing and what is going on with them. Statements such as, "Are you all right?" and "Can I help with anything?" let students know they are cared for, valued, and noticed.

Listening intently and sincerely to students is a powerful way to communicate how much you care. Maintaining eye contact and paraphrasing helps students realize that you have heard them.

In addition, when you *empathize with students,* they understand that they are recognized and valued. This does not mean that you have to agree with all their actions, but that you let them know that you recognize the emotions behind their actions. You can communicate empathy by telling students that even though it's wrong to hit someone, for instance, you understand the emotions behind an incident.

These are just a few ways that you can demonstrate to your students that you care about them. As indicated earlier, you must never forget the power of caring. The bottom line is that caring helps build strong positive relationships that in turn help prevent discipline problems in the future.

Preventing and Reducing Frustration and Stress

Frustration and stress, which are inevitable in the teaching profession, are the great enemies of our best intentions. Zehm and Kottler (1993) list some external causes of stress for teachers as difficult students, irate parents, and collegial backbiting. Frustration can have a devastating effect on teacher-student relationships, as it tends to cause educators to make irrational decisions. Usually you know when you are becoming frustrated and can quickly identify the signs and symptoms. As an educator, the question is not *if* you will become frustrated or stressed but *when* you will and *how* you will deal with it.

Signs of frustration or stress can include nervousness, anxiety, shortness of breath, and a tendency to make irrational decisions. First, you should be able to recognize your own personal signs that frustration or stress is building so that you can de-escalate them. You should then have a plan that will help you prevent or reduce frustration when it occurs. Your frustration prevention or reduction techniques will be unique and personal to you; what works for one teacher might not necessarily be effective for you. Figure 1.8 shows some typical frustration and stress prevention or reduction techniques that you can implement.

FIGURE 1.8

FRUSTRATION AND STRESS PREVENTION/REDUCTION TECHNIQUES

- Play soft, relaxing music
- Display posters of peaceful destinations
- Modify your lesson plans
- Take your students for a walk
- Ask a neighboring teacher to take a difficult student for a period of time
- Assign your students independent reading time
- Clear off your desk
- Find a validating colleague
- Share staff duties
- Share frustration strategies

Playing soft, relaxing music when feelings of frustration are approaching can have a beneficial effect for both you and your students. Some teachers proactively play soft music during independent study time.

Displaying posters throughout the classroom of attractive destinations can help keep you calm. You might put up pictures of beautiful beaches, snowy mountains, green valleys, ski resorts, or tropical islands to give yourself—and your students—opportunities for mini mental vacations.

Most teachers have certain lessons they truly enjoy teaching. When feelings of frustration or stress are approaching, try *modifying your lesson plans* and teaching a lesson that not only meets the student learning goals but also brings you pleasure.

Sometimes just *taking a short walk* around the school can be relaxing and can head off feelings of stress or frustration. This can also help students relieve pent-up energy. For instance, there may even be a way to integrate the walk into your current curriculum by turning it into a nature walk or a service project (e.g., picking up litter).

Difficult students can be a major cause of frustration. Allow yourself to ask for help by *asking a neighboring teacher to take a difficult student for a short time*. This strategy is one that you should set up ahead of time, making certain that your colleague is agreeable to this arrangement. Offering to do the same for the other teacher is a good way to begin using this strategy.

Strategically *assigning independent reading time to students* is another way to calm the classroom down and provide you with a break when frustration raises its ugly head.

For some teachers, one source of stress or frustration is a messy desk, submerged in various unfinished tasks. If you are one of these teachers, an easy way to decrease frustration is to *clear off your desk* and take time to organize your work area.

Frustration and stress often disappear when a supervisor or peer lets you know they value and appreciate your work. Knowing which colleagues you should visit to help *validate your work* is another technique to use in lowering levels of frustration and stress. *Sharing staff duties* can help too, as frustration and stress often occur when a teacher feels overwhelmed and behind. You should let your colleagues know you are willing to cover some of their duties and also let them do the same for you. Also, *sharing other ideas* with teachers on frustration- and stress-reducing techniques is a way to increase your repertoire of strategies.

Zehm and Kottler (1993) mention additional stress- and frustration-reduction strategies, such as maintaining a healthy lifestyle with good sleeping patterns, free of alcohol and drugs. They also advocate continued training and professional growth tasks, such as varying teaching assignments, taking a sabbatical, having a faculty exchange, engaging in team teaching, supervising a student teacher, going back to school, conducting field trips, leading research projects, writing grants, and instigating technology projects. In addition, they suggest keeping a journal as a reflective strategy to help deal with stress and frustration.

In summary, there are many ways you can develop positive relationships with students in your daily interactions with them. Not only does this contribute to a positive classroom environment, but it also improves the quality of school life for both you and your students.

While building positive relationships is the foundation to a strong discipline system, relationships alone are not enough. It is also critical to clearly define parameters of expected behaviors, to monitor those behaviors, and to implement consequences when necessary.

2

Establishing Clearly Defined Parameters of Acceptable Classroom Behaviors

Establishing and teaching clearly defined parameters of acceptable behaviors is a critical part of classroom discipline, making up approximately 25 percent of the overall picture (see Figure S1). In a summary of the research on classroom management, Marzano (2003) found that "across the various grade levels the average number of disruptions in classes where rules and procedures were effectively implemented was 28 percentile points lower than the average number of disruptions in classes where that was not the case" (p. 14).

Every teacher should formally take the time to teach and enforce clearly defined parameters of acceptable student behaviors. Unfortunately, many teachers make the mistake of announcing rather than teaching parameters to their students. The truth is that students do not learn what's announced; they learn what they are taught. It makes no more sense to announce rules regarding acceptable student behaviors than it does to announce—rather than teach—math facts. It is critical that you formally teach and enforce both a discipline plan and rules of conduct from the very first day of school.

What are the differences between the discipline plan and rules of conduct? Canter and Canter (1997) describe a discipline plan as an umbrella policy that specifies rules that apply to all students, at all times, in all locations. A discipline plan also specifies how you will respond when students comply or fail to comply with the rules.

Canter and Canter (1997) also describe rules of conduct as the policies and rules that apply to specific classroom and buildingwide locations and events, such as attending assemblies, working with substitutes, getting drinks, and using the pencil sharpener. In the category that we call "rules of conduct," Marzano (2003) includes how to begin and end the class day or period; make transitions to bathrooms; conduct fire drills; use the library; go to a specialist; distribute, use, and store special equipment; conduct group work; and behave when doing seat work and during teacher-led activities, including what to do when work is finished. He states that clearly defined and taught procedures decrease disciplinary problems at all grade levels.

You must take whatever time is needed to teach both the discipline plan and the rules of conduct as they apply to your class. If you do not formally teach these concepts, students will be confused as they attempt to determine what the acceptable policies and procedures are for the classroom. Also, students who have not been taught rules for acceptable behaviors may test the waters to find out how far they can push the envelope. Investing time in communicating and teaching your classroom discipline plan and rules of conduct is extremely worthwhile, as it ultimately yields increased learning time for all students.

Discipline Plan

Your discipline plan should encompass all rules for all students in all locations. The list should not be too long; that is, five or six rules should be the maximum. Following these six steps will help you to implement an effective discipline plan in your classroom:

1. Select rules that are meaningful, specific, and enforceable. Rules such as "Students are to be good at all times" and "Students are to act responsibly at all times" are inappropriate because they are too vague and open to misinterpretation.
2. Establish consequences for students who fail to comply with the discipline plan.
3. Teach the discipline plan to the students.
4. Post the discipline plan in an easily seen classroom location.
5. Communicate the discipline plan to parents and the principal.
6. Enforce the discipline plan fairly, consistently, and equitably.

Be sure that the rules outlined in your discipline plan are appropriate, as in Step 1 above. Take a look at the following rules and consider how difficult they would be to enforce:

- Be good at all times.
- Act maturely.
- Act appropriately.
- Be kind.

While these rules apply to all students in all locations, they are stated in such a general manner that they can be interpreted differently by different students. In contrast, the rules in the next list not only apply to all students in all locations, but are also specific enough to be understood by all students:

- Follow teacher directives.
- Follow all rules of conduct.
- Speak quietly.
- Keep your hands to yourselves.

Even though these rules are more specific, there still may need to be some clarification of terms. For example, what you mean by "speaking quietly" may need to be taught and demonstrated so that your students are clear on what that means to you. Model what "quietly" is and is not, and have students demonstrate their understanding. This is especially important at the elementary grade levels. The point is to use words that have as little variability in interpretation as possible and, when necessary, to teach exactly what is meant by the rules so that everyone is clear about classroom expectations.

Rules of Conduct

Your rules of conduct should clearly let students know what the specific behavior standards are for various classroom and building locations and activities. Canter and Canter (1997) recommend that there be three categories of rules of conduct: academic, classroom, and special situation.

Academic rules of conduct prescribe specific behaviors that are expected during academics. These may include rules regarding the following:

- Expectations for participating in class discussions

- Expectations for seat work activities
- What students should bring to class to be prepared
- How to seek the teacher's assistance
- When, where, and how to turn in completed work

Rather than simply post academic rules of conduct, you should teach them to your students in the context of specific academic situations. For example, when conducting class discussions, you could teach students that you expect them to raise their hands and be called on to take part in discussions, you expect everyone to participate, and you expect students to be respectful by listening attentively to the thoughts and opinions of others.

When teaching expectations for seat work activities, you could instruct the students on how to get help if needed, when and how to get necessary materials, when and how to sharpen their pencils, and what to do after their work is completed. In training students how to come to class prepared to work, you could teach your students to bring the books needed for the specific subject, pencils or pens, paper or a notebook, and any special equipment, such as calculators. Each teacher needs to determine what items students require to be prepared in his or her class and must teach the students to bring their supplies on a consistent basis so that they can be ready to learn with the fewest disruptions to instruction.

Another element you should teach students under your academic rules of conduct is how to seek your assistance. This may vary depending on the grouping status of your classroom; the rules for seeking assistance will probably be different if you are working with small student groups than if all students are doing independent work or working in cooperative groups. In some situations, you may expect them to ask another student before coming to you for help. You may require that they use other strategies, such as seeking help from the dictionary or just making their best guesses without assistance. Different situations may call for students coming up to your desk, raising their hands, or using a "help" card to signal that they need help. The point is that you should clearly teach your expectations in the context of various academic situations, depending on the special academic setting and what you determine will help an individual student and not interfere with other students' learning.

When, where, and how to turn in completed work is another academic rule of conduct that you should teach to your students. If you want students to turn in homework assignments by placing them in the homework basket at the beginning of the class period before they are seated, it is important that you teach that and consistently reinforce students for doing it correctly. If students are doing independent seat work and you want them to wait until the bell rings to turn in their work to you on their way out the door, you need to teach that. What you want them to do with completed work is not as important as your teaching what you want within the context of the specific situation. Again, we stress that students learn what is taught, not what is simply announced.

Figure 2.1 is an example of academic rules of conduct you may want to include in your classroom.

FIGURE 2.1

ACADEMIC RULES OF CONDUCT

Class discussions:
- Raise your hand
- Wait to be called on
- Listen attentively and respectfully
- Everyone is to participate

Seat work activities:
- Hold up "help" card for help
- Clear your desk of unneeded supplies
- Sharpen pencils when you enter the classroom
- Read a book when work is completed

Coming to class prepared:
- Bring books needed for the subject
- Bring pencils or pens
- Bring paper, a notebook, and a calculator

How to seek assistance:
- Hold up "help" card during independent work
- Ask your neighbor during reading groups for help

Completed work:
- Place in designated baskets at the teacher's direction

Homework:
- Place in designated baskets when entering classroom at the start of class

---

Classroom rules of conduct prescribe specific behaviors that are expected while students are in the classroom and procedures that students are to follow. They include expectations about the following kinds of activities:

- When to use the pencil sharpener
- How, when, and where to get drinks
- How to enter and exit the classroom
- How to respond to the teacher's signal
- What constitutes a tardy

Once again, rather than simply posting these rules, you should teach them on the first day of school and reteach as necessary. It is critical that your instruction be specific regarding your expectations and that you consistently hold students accountable to these expectations.

You may allow students to use the pencil sharpener only at the beginning of the school day or during independent seat work so as not to interfere with instruction. The same may apply to when you want students to get drinks. Some teachers expect and teach their students specific ways to enter the classroom, such as lining up at the door before being given permission to enter. When students do come in, you may expect them to go directly to their seats and work on the assignment on the board. Many teachers insist that at the end of class, the bell does not excuse the students, the teacher does. In order for this to be done in an orderly fashion, students may be excused one row at a time, with the teacher waiting until the entire row of students is ready and quiet before excusing them.

Regarding the teacher's signal, it is essential that the students know what the signal is, that they give the teacher their attention immediately when the signal is given, and that the teacher wait until every student has complied before continuing. And finally, teachers must teach what they mean by "tardy," whether it commences immediately after the bell rings or up to a minute after the bell rings.

Again, we are advocating not that you adopt these specific procedures for your classroom rules of conduct but that you decide what your rules are and then teach and reinforce them for your students. Figure 2.2 lists examples of classroom rules of conduct.

FIGURE 2.2

CLASSROOM RULES OF CONDUCT

Pencil sharpener:
- Use before the tardy bell

Drinks:
- Get before the tardy bell

Entering the classroom:
- Line up at the door, and wait for the teacher to admit you to the classroom

Exiting the classroom:
- Clear desks
- Sit quietly
- Keep eyes on the teacher
- Wait for dismissal by the teacher

Response to teacher's signal:
- Keep hands folded
- Sit quietly
- Keep eyes on the teacher

Arrival to class:
- Be in your seat before the tardy bell rings

Special situation rules of conduct prescribe behaviors that are expected when students participate in special activities. They include rules about the following procedures:
- How to go to the library or gym
- How to work with substitutes
- How to respond to fire drills

Students going to the library or gym may be expected to follow dismissal procedures similar to those at the end of the day, with students waiting for the teacher to line them up rather than running to the door when the bell rings. Many teachers teach their students that whatever rules apply when the teacher is there also remain in effect when there is a substitute teacher in the classroom. As additional support, they may make consequences for student misbehaviors harsher when a substitute is in charge. When you teach your students how to respond to fire drills, you may have them immediately stop whatever they are doing, quickly and quietly walk to and line up in the designated area, and silently wait for instructions.

Figure 2.3 shows examples of special situation rules of conduct that you may have for your classroom.

FIGURE 2.3

SPECIAL SITUATION RULES OF CONDUCT

Going to the library, the gym, lunch, or a specialist:
  • Wait to be dismissed by the teacher
  • Walk quietly and quickly to line up
  • Wait silently

Substitutes:
  • All building and classroom rules apply with substitutes

Fire drills:
  • Stop what you are doing immediately
  • Be silent
  • Walk quietly and quickly to the designated area
  • Wait for the teacher's instructions

Whatever you decide on for your rules of conduct, there are five steps you should follow in establishing these rules:

1. Determine the rules of conduct for each category.
2. Teach the rules of conduct.
3. Post the rules of conduct.
4. Communicate the rules of conduct to parents and the principal.
5. Enforce the rules of conduct by implementing the consequences that are specified in your discipline plan.

Joanna is a 1st grade teacher. She firmly believes that students need to follow clearly defined parameters of acceptable classroom behaviors. On the first day of school, she taught students her signal and how to respond to it, what supplies to bring to class every day, how to be dismissed from class, where to put their work, when to sharpen their pencils, and how to get help from the teacher. Not only did she teach these rules to the students, but throughout the day they practiced the rules and she posted them clearly and visibly on the walls of the classroom. She knew that she would spend at least the first couple of weeks of school teaching these rules and practicing them with her students until the students' compliance became automatic. In addition, she had communicated all of her classroom rules to the principal and to the parents in a letter that she sent home before the first day of school. In that letter, she included her classroom phone number and the best times for parents to call if they had any questions. She also reviewed the consequences that would ensue if students failed to follow the classroom rules and the positive rewards for following the rules.

Teaching Your Discipline Plan and Rules of Conduct

Remember, the time you spend teaching both your discipline plan and your rules of conduct is an investment that pays huge dividends in increased learning, on-task student behavior, and increased job satisfaction for you. This is a very important concept, one that many teachers fail to spend adequate time addressing. This could be due to the following misconceptions many teachers have regarding teaching a discipline plan, as Jones (1987) points out:

- Kids should just know the rules.
- Rules only need to be announced.
- Rules only need to be taught at the beginning of the year.
- Kids resent time spent teaching and enforcing rules.

The truth is that if you don't teach the rules, your students won't know what the rules are and they will test you. Also, as we stated earlier, students learn what they are taught, not what is announced. This needs to be an ongoing process, with the rules taught and retaught as needed, not just at the beginning of the year. Finally, students don't resent the time spent on this process. They want structure, and structure is needed in order to provide good instruction.

You should follow these six steps when teaching your discipline plan and rules of conduct:

1. *Begin with a set.* Begin the lesson by clearly communicating to the students what they are about to learn and why it is important.
2. *Explain the logic and rationale for each rule.* Students tend to support policies that are logical and make sense. Don't assume the students understand the logic behind each rule. Instead, explain the rationale for each rule and why it's important.
3. *Model the behavior that is expected.* The best lessons incorporate specific examples of the concepts being taught. When teaching

your discipline plan and rules of conduct, you should model exactly what is expected.

4. *Allow for questions and answers.* Encourage your students to ask questions to be certain they understand the concepts being taught.

5. *Direct students to demonstrate their understanding.* After you teach both your discipline plan and rules of conduct, you should require the students to demonstrate their understanding of the concepts. The students should be required to repeatedly practice the rules until it is clear they grasp them.

6. *Reteach the discipline plan and rules of conduct.* If at any time it becomes apparent that the students are not abiding by your discipline plan or rules of conduct, you should not hesitate to reteach each of the concepts.

Thomas is a new 5th grade teacher. He understands that he needs to be very clear with his students regarding what he expects and to explain the rationale for his expectations. One of the rules he has for his students is that they walk very quietly and respectfully in the hallways when transitioning from the classroom to other parts of the school, such as for lunch, for assemblies, or to go to the library. On the first day of school, he explains that the class will receive instruction not only in the classroom but also in many different parts of the school building. He goes on to make clear to the class that as the oldest grade level in the building, they are responsible for modeling appropriate behavior for other students. In addition, he tells them that he has confidence in them, is proud of them, and knows that they will be a shining example for the entire school. He goes on to explain that when they are moving from one place to another, there is a potential for other classrooms to be interrupted and disturbed if students walking in the hallways are loud or inconsiderate. He expects his students to walk in a straight line on the right side of the hallway, be absolutely silent when they walk, and keep their hands to themselves. He demonstrates what he means with a couple of students he has "pretaught," and he then has the class practice several times during the day.

An excellent way to see how well the students understand your discipline plan and rules of conduct is to give them a written test. Thompson (1998) encourages teachers to give students a test that requires them to answer questions regarding the classroom and building discipline plan and rules of conduct. Figure 2.4 shows some questions teachers might want to put on the test.

FIGURE 2.4

DISCIPLINE PLAN TEST

- List four things you are to do when you hear, "Give me your attention, please."
- List the procedures you must follow before using the bathroom.
- List two things you must do to avoid being tardy.
- What are the four items you are to bring to class always?
- List the two times you are allowed to go to your locker.

Setting and teaching clearly established parameters for acceptable student behaviors is an important component of a discipline plan. When they are done effectively and monitored closely, consequences rarely need to be used.

■ ■ ■

3

Putting Monitoring Skills into Practice

Developing monitoring skills is crucial to the success of your classroom discipline plan. The ability to effectively monitor your students' behaviors is one of the most powerful discipline tools available to you, as well as one of the best ways to prevent incipient classroom discipline problems from growing. Keen monitoring skills will enable you to communicate to students that you are aware of what they are doing and that any inappropriate behavior needs to stop at once, and to do this in a manner that does not hinder or disrupt your instruction. Also, the appropriate use of monitoring skills promotes positive changes in students' behaviors while allowing students to keep their dignity.

As illustrated in Figure S1, monitoring skills make up approximately 25 percent of an effective discipline plan. Along with positive teacher-student relationships and the establishment of clear parameters of acceptable student behaviors, the employment of monitoring skills is a proactive strategy that can prevent student misbehaviors from escalating to the point where disciplinary consequences are necessary.

Jones (1987) summarizes the results of thousands of classroom observations in which teachers' disciplinary interventions with students were tallied. These results make it apparent that teachers rarely had to intervene with students as a result of profanity or fighting. In fact, Jones stated that if the only classroom disciplinary interventions teachers needed to deal with involved fighting and profanity, they would spend very little time on discipline. His study indicated that 95 percent of teachers' interventions involved issues related to talking out of turn in the classroom and out-of-seat behaviors. His conclusions were that there are three major reasons why students get out of their seats or speak out inappropriately in the classroom:

- The student thinks the teacher does not see the behavior.
- The student thinks the teacher does not care about the behavior.
- The student thinks there will be no significant consequence for the behavior.

When teachers employ monitoring skills, they communicate that they do see the behavior and are concerned about the behavior and that it is not in a student's best interest to continue with this inappropriate behavior.

Thompson (1998) defines monitoring as being "acutely aware of what each student is doing every minute of the class. It requires the hyper-alert-ness of a combat veteran. . . . It's the famous 'eyes in the back of your head' that is the hallmark of excellent teachers who can write on the chalk-board and tell a student in the back of the room to stop passing notes at the same time" (p. 165). Marzano (2003) defines monitoring as "withitness . . . . remaining 'with it' (aware of what is happening in all parts of the class-room at all times) by continuously scanning the classroom, even when working with small groups or individuals" (p. 67).

Four monitoring skills that should become part of your repertoire are maintaining proximity, invoking silence, providing response opportunities, and practicing the "teacher's look." The fifth skill is the ability to use all these monitoring skills simultaneously. Let's look at each of these monitoring skills in more detail.

Maintaining Proximity

One of the best ways to let students know they are being watched is by maintaining a close proximity to them—being physically within five feet of them. The magical effect of this skill is that students "feel" your presence and alter their behaviors accordingly. Moving toward a student who is starting to get off task is a quick and easy way to silently communicate the message that he or she needs to get back to work immediately. Also, you can easily maintain a close proximity without interrupting your instruc-tion. Some teachers are so tied to the front of the room that they rarely move around. It is important to remember that "good things happen" when you are close to your students. There is nothing wrong with conducting your lesson from a variety of classroom locations. In fact, routinely changing where they stand while leading their classes is a strategy some teachers use regularly to monitor different groups of students.

It is good instructional practice to examine your personal proximity patterns. When you do this, you might discover certain areas of the classroom that you typically ignore, such as a back corner, the middle, or a front corner. Marzano (2003) states that teachers should spend time in each quadrant of the room as they walk around; this can proactively head off disciplinary issues. Often the ignored areas of the classroom are where the most disruptive and off-task students sit. Moving disruptive students to locations where you can maintain proximity or changing your proximity patterns are ways to deal with the issue. The first step in the use of this strategy, however, is to analyze what you are currently doing. Use a video recording of your instruction or enlist the help of a fellow teacher or your principal to record your movements.

In the proximity chart shown in Figure 3.1, an observer used an "X" to mark where the teacher was every 30 seconds during classroom instruction. In this example, it is clear that the teacher is avoiding the center of the classroom, thereby missing opportunities to maintain proximity to the students sitting near the center. After analyzing the chart, the teacher may decide to change this pattern.

FIGURE 3.1

PROXIMITY CHART

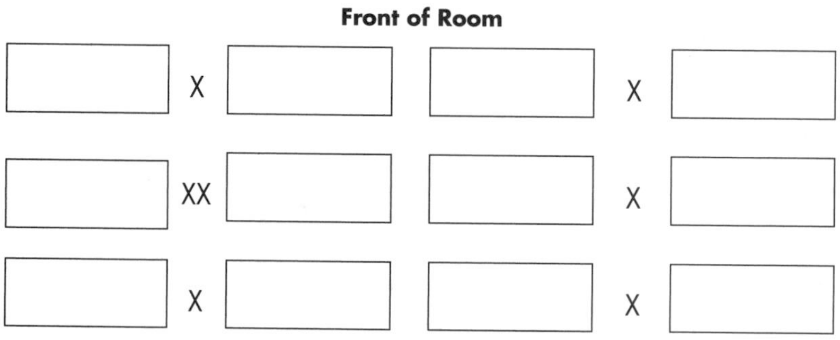

Front of Room

Watching for students who are beginning to get off task and moving toward them before the problem escalates is a very effective strategy. Maintaining proximity in this way can quickly stop inappropriate behaviors from getting worse. There really is no bad time to use this skill. Staying close to your students during both your direct instruction and independent seat work helps to keep them on task and attentive. It also gives you a great opportunity to monitor students' academic performance and give them immediate, specific feedback.

Invoking Silence

Often the loudest sound you can hear in a classroom is silence. In fact, silence can be an immediate way to get the students' attention. When you suddenly break your instruction flow and implement a protracted silence, students who are beginning to get off task or become disruptive will often get back on task.

A key time for an extended silence is after students are given instructions. After making a statement such as, "Turn to page 16" or "Take out your reading books," you should monitor the students and make sure that they are following your instructions. Each statement should be followed by a silence that lasts until every student takes part in the activity. Also remember that a 10-second silence can seem like an eternity to students. There are few strategies that are so easy to use and so powerful as invoking silence.

Providing Response Opportunities

Many students tend to get off task during classroom discussions because the teacher fails to hold them accountable for what is being discussed. If your instructional style communicates that certain students will not be asked to participate in the discussion, there is an increased likelihood those students will tune out.

An effective way to maintain on-task student behavior during teacher-led discussions is to provide response opportunities to as many students as possible. Requiring choral responses and directing every student to write answers to your questions on scratch paper are a couple of ways to keep all students thinking about the concepts being discussed. Keep in mind that when you exclusively call on students who have their hands raised, you are inadvertently increasing the likelihood that students with their hands down will lose their focus on the class's activity and not think about the topic of discussion. One way to ensure that you call on students equitably is to have all of their names in a box and randomly pull out a name, thereby indicating who should answer a question.

The key is to increase response opportunities for each and every student. Remember that every time you call on a student, you are communicating the message that he or she is a part of the class and will be held accountable for what is being taught. Also, be careful not to fall into the trap of never calling on a student because you are worried that he or she will be embarrassed or humiliated. A far greater danger is that by failing to call on a student, you give him or her tacit permission to go off task and tune out.

Practicing "The Look"

Experienced teachers often make use of a powerful tool known as "the look." Looking intently at a student who is beginning to get off task can quickly draw his or her attention back to the matter at hand. This type of look communicates that you are aware of what the student is doing and that you wish the undesirable behavior to stop.

Marzano (2003) reinforces this strategy by encouraging teachers, as they periodically scan the room, to make eye contact with students and to pay attention to situations that look as though they could escalate into problems.

Using All These Skills Simultaneously

For some students, having a teacher in close proximity is all that is needed to get them back on task. For others, providing a response opportunity, giving them a "look," or invoking a moment of silence may be required. In some cases, you may decide to use all four of these monitoring strategies at one time.

Here's an example of what that might look like. Mike is getting off task and beginning to be slightly disruptive while you are teaching a math lesson. You suddenly stop your instruction, look directly at Mike, and say,

"Mike, what's the answer to that last question?" After he looks at you blankly, you walk up to him as you continue to hold his attention, and quietly say, "Mike, I'll be back." This can be a very effective way to make your point, get the student back on task, and decrease the chances of a similar situation happening again.

Using all of the monitoring strategies at one time with a single student relays an extremely powerful message. You should be careful, therefore, about when and with whom you use all the strategies together. With some students, this might be overkill and could even be counterproductive, resulting in an outburst. The key is to know your students and understand with whom you should use the combined strategies and with whom you should not.

The important point to remember with monitoring skills is that the most effective discipline approaches are immediate, powerful, easily implemented, and minimally disruptive to the instructional process. Monitoring incorporates all of these characteristics. When monitoring is not enough, however, teachers need to have meaningful, immediate consequences at their disposal. The next chapter addresses effective consequences a teacher can use with students.

4

Implementing Consequences

Consequences to misbehaviors will be necessary when other approaches are unsuccessful. They are the most negative part of a teacher's job, and when overused they often lack the desired impact. The best discipline plans strive to limit the need for punishments and negative consequences by having a preventive emphasis. Developing positive teacher-student relations, establishing clear parameters of acceptable behaviors, and using monitoring strategies are extremely effective preventive approaches to discipline, but they are not always enough to ensure appropriate student behavior.

Using their own resources, teachers can implement a range of consequences when students misbehave, including warnings, student conferences, parent conferences, and lunch detentions or after-school detentions run by the teacher. These punishments are readily available to all teachers in all schools because individual teachers can carry them out regardless of support from the building administration. Marzano (2003) categorizes interventions that individual teachers can use into five groups:

- *Teacher reaction:* verbal and physical behaviors of teachers that indicate to students that their behavior is appropriate or inappropriate
- *Tangible recognition:* strategies in which students are provided with some symbol or token for appropriate behavior
- *Direct cost:* interventions that involve a direct and concrete consequence for misbehavior
- *Group contingency:* a specific set of students must reach a certain criterion level or appropriate behavior

- *Home contingency*: behavior monitoring occurs at a student's home (pp. 29–30)

Unfortunately, while these interventions are important and necessary, they often do not provide teachers with the diversity, effectiveness, or immediacy that buildingwide support systems can. It is important that schools empower teachers by enabling them to choose from a variety of strategies regarding student discipline. The best way to be certain that teachers have a number of meaningful and effective consequences that they can use to counteract misbehavior is for the administration and school staff to work together to set up buildingwide support systems. Consequences that require buildingwide support systems include processing, lunch detentions, after-school detentions, Friday school detentions, and office referrals. We will address these in the next section.

End of Section Reflection Questions

1. What are the components that make up a discipline plan?
2. Which component(s) do you rely on the most? Which component(s) would you like to add to your discipline toolbox? If this requires an adjustment in your style, how will you accomplish this?
3. Which strategies are you going to add to your repertoire from each of the discipline component areas?
4. What is the most important concept(s) you learned from this section?

BUILDINGWIDE
DISCIPLINE

Buildingwide Discipline

There is a strong relationship between classroom discipline and building-wide discipline. In fact, classroom discipline is the "driver" of building discipline because students spend the majority of their day in the classroom and often take the discipline culture from the classroom with them to the rest of the building. Marzano (2003) states that buildingwide discipline is as important as classroom management and may even contribute more to the climate of the school.

The strategies that are needed to establish and maintain an orderly and structured buildingwide environment are the same strategies used within the classroom. And the expectations for student behavior throughout the school should be consistent with classroom expectations.

The establishment and maintenance of a structured and orderly environment is just as important outside of the classroom as it is inside the classroom. Staff members should make a commitment to implement discipline strategies that will ensure structure and order throughout the entire building (hallways, office, fields, bus zones, etc.). In this section, a strong case will be made for concentrating on the establishment of a structured building environment through a systems approach. Also, specific strategies for doing this will be explained.

In order for systems of consequences to be established that are varied, immediate, meaningful, and easy to use, the entire staff must work together. While setting up such a system buildingwide initially takes a great deal of coordination and cooperation, once it is in place, teachers will be empowered to address student misbehaviors and classroom time can be used more efficiently.

The foundation of developing buildingwide discipline systems comes from some core philosophical beliefs. In the next chapter, we will examine those beliefs.

5

Philosophical Beliefs

To create an effective buildingwide discipline plan, the entire staff must embrace a common philosophy. It is important not only to initially discuss and develop the building philosophy as an entire staff, but also to review the philosophy and building rules together on a regular basis as a way to continually bring new staff on board and to recalibrate the philosophy.

A strong buildingwide discipline philosophy comprises six major points:

1. *Chaos outside the classroom will spill into the classroom.* If students are disruptive prior to entering the classroom, they will bring those behaviors with them into the classroom. Teachers will then need to take their time to settle the students down and get them into a learning mode. This diverts valuable time from instruction.

2. *Pay now or pay later.* If school staff fail to lay the groundwork for effective discipline at the beginning of the year, they will pay the price with disruptive classroom and schoolwide environments later, at which time it will be much more difficult to address the problem. It is crucial that the entire building staff work together to set parameters and enforce expectations immediately and consistently from the first day of school in order to prevent future problems.

3. *A chaotic school environment is destructive to the school climate.* When students are disruptive in the hallways, office, fields, assemblies, bus zones, or any other building location, the school's reputation, the level of parent support, student learning, and staff morale are dramatically affected.

4. *Strategies that work in the classroom also work outside of the classroom.* The same components of a classroom discipline plan—positive teacher-student relations, clear parameters, monitoring skills, and the use of meaningful consequences—that help teachers create a structured classroom environment are also effective buildingwide.

5. *Creating a structured building environment is not easy.* Although developing and maintaining a supportive and orderly buildingwide environment involves a lot of work on the part of the administration and school staff, the payoff will be significant.

6. *Everyone must do his or her part.* Buildingwide structure cannot be established unless each staff member makes a contribution. Counselors, teachers, administrators, para-educators, custodians, and librarians all must own the effort to create a structured and orderly environment. No staff member should think his or her job does not include supporting the buildingwide discipline plan.

The next chapter outlines buildingwide prevention strategies that can establish and maintain positive buildingwide discipline and help teachers and administrators avoid the need for implementing negative consequences for student misbehaviors.

6

Buildingwide Prevention Strategies

Developing strategies that can be used on a buildingwide basis to prevent discipline problems requires teamwork to select the best approach for your school and to work on it with consistency throughout the building. There is no one-size-fits-all approach to discipline, so you must determine which are the best techniques for your school. Keep in mind that if the building-wide discipline plan emphasizes prevention, there will be fewer rule violations; if the system neglects preventive strategies, there is a potential for a multitude of rule violations.

Let's look at some strategies that can be used on a buildingwide basis to prevent behavior problems.

Discipline Assessment

As a preventive strategy, buildingwide discipline should be regularly and proactively addressed before major discipline issues can occur. Too many schools put off examining their discipline policies and procedures until problems get out of control. Buildingwide discipline is too important to "put on the shelf." At the beginning of every school year, staff should reevaluate their discipline system. During grade-level, cabinet, and staff meetings, there should be regular opportunities for staff to review and assess all aspects of the school's disciplinary procedures. Staff members should be encouraged to bring up any areas of concern or ideas for improvement.

Using a brainstorming approach is a great way to get to the important issues regarding discipline. First, all staff should brainstorm any concerns they have regarding building discipline issues. These can be listed in a prominent place for all to see, such as on a flip chart. Second, each staff member should be given an opportunity to advocate, for up to 30 seconds, on the top issue he or she feels must be dealt with and why, with the rest of the staff quietly listening and refraining from comment. And finally, the concerns should be prioritized by each staff member, with everyone given a specific number of votes to spread across their top issues. The top-ranking items then can be worked on by a discipline committee, which will bring recommendations back to the staff.

Involving the entire staff in the process is critical; such involvement builds ownership, helps staff understand the rationale for each rule so that they can communicate the rationales to students, and increases the chance that the entire staff will support the policies. When only a couple of people develop buildingwide policies, the likelihood that the whole staff will support them and follow through with students decreases.

Another way to assess the buildingwide discipline system is to conduct a formal staff survey. A formal staff survey should be given to every certificated and classified employee at least once a year. The survey should request feedback on all aspects of the buildingwide discipline system. This can then be used as information on how to make effective changes to the plan. Figure 6.1 shows an example of a buildingwide discipline survey.

FIGURE 6.1

BUILDINGWIDE DISCIPLINE SYSTEM SURVEY—STAFF

Scoring instructions: Score each statement on a scale of 1 to 10 using the following scale: We do well = 10; We do OK = 5–9; We need to do much better = 1–4

1. Our staff is committed to recognizing student achievement and developing pride in success.
   Score: _____
2. Our entire staff does a good job of enforcing the agreed-upon building rules and policies.
   Score: _____
3. Our staff has access to quick, meaningful, and easy-to-implement consequences to student misbehaviors.
   Score: _____
4. Our staff makes timely parent contacts regarding student discipline.
   Score: _____
5. Our building administrators do not hesitate to contact parents when concerns develop.
   Score: _____

(Figure continued on next page)

FIGURE 6.1

BUILDINGWIDE DISCIPLINE SYSTEM SURVEY—STAFF (CONTINUED)

6. Our building administration gives teachers timely feedback after students are referred to the office.
Score: _____
7. Our building administrators employ quick and meaningful consequences when students are referred to the office.
Score: _____
8. Our staff is visible and seen by the students in all building locations throughout the day.
Score: _____
9. The buildingwide rules have been introduced and taught to the students.
Score: _____
10. Our staff has regular opportunities to review and discuss the building's discipline system and procedures.
Score: _____
11. Our staff has an "it takes a village" approach when students disobey a rule or policy.
Score: _____
12. Our staff realizes that enforcing buildingwide discipline is everyone's responsibility.
Score: _____
13. When we have discipline concerns, we know that the administration will back us.
Score: _____
14. Our office is not filled with kids who are in trouble.
Score: _____
15. Other issues:
Score: _____

To get a complete and valid assessment of your school's discipline system, it is a good idea to survey parents as well as staff. Figure 6.2 gives an example of a parent discipline system survey.

FIGURE 6.2

BUILDINGWIDE DISCIPLINE SYSTEM SURVEY—PARENTS

Scoring instructions: Score each statement on a scale of 1 to 10 using the following scale: We do well = 10; We do OK = 5–9; We need to do much better = 1–4

1. The staff is committed to recognizing student achievement and developing pride in success.
Score: _____
2. The staff does a good job of enforcing the agreed-upon buildingwide rules and policies.
Score: _____

(Figure continued on next page)

FIGURE 6.2

BUILDINGWIDE DISCIPLINE SYSTEM SURVEY—PARENTS

(CONTINUED)

3. The staff makes timely parent contacts regarding student discipline.
   Score: _____
4. The building administrators do not hesitate to contact parents when concerns develop.
   Score: _____
5. The building administrators give quick and meaningful consequences when students are referred to the office.
   Score: _____
6. The staff is visible and seen by the students and parents in all building locations throughout the day.
   Score: _____
7. The buildingwide rules have been communicated to the parents.
   Score: _____
8. The office is not filled with kids who are in trouble.
   Score: _____
9. Other issues:
   Score: _____

Sunnyside High School in Sunnyside, Washington, developed a matrix for staff members to evaluate themselves on how well they communicate high expectations and how effectively they communicate and consistently implement rules and policies. In Figure 6.3, we have adapted this matrix to show another tool that can be used to assess how well individuals are supporting the buildingwide discipline philosophy and rules.

FIGURE 6.3

STAFF SELF-ASSESSMENT OF DISCIPLINE/
STUDENT RELATIONSHIP INTERACTION

	4	3	2	1
Communication	Equity in communicated expectation: sincere compliments, written and verbal encouragement	Periodic verbal/written encouragement with most students	Encouragement of a small number of students	None; sarcasm used as personal discipline

(Figure continued on next page)

FIGURE 6.3

STAFF SELF-ASSESSMENT OF DISCIPLINE/
STUDENT RELATIONSHIP INTERACTION (CONTINUED)

	4	3	2	1
Expectations/ Guidelines	4 Rules posted, reviewed, taught, and consistently enforced	3 Rules posted and periodically enforced	2 Rules posted but not enforced or enforced but not posted	1 Rules not posted and not consistently enforced
Discipline	4 Consistent adherence to school policies and procedures	3 Adherence to most policies and procedures	2 Adherence to some policies and procedures	1 Rare adherence to policies and discipline is not positive

Variations to the left of the dotted line are ideal.
Variations to the left of the solid line are acceptable.
Variations to the right of the solid line are unacceptable.

Support of the Policies

No staff member should think that he or she is above supporting the buildingwide rules. There are a number of things that happen when staff members fail to support building policies:

- Overall staff morale drops dramatically.
- Staff members who do support the rules become upset with those who do not.
- Students know who will let them break the rules.
- The entire discipline system is undermined.

There are a number of ways that staff can support the school's discipline policies. Minimally, all staff should support the policies by covering assigned duties, monitoring rule violations, and keeping an eye on all students, not just their own.

Ensuring buildingwide policy support is a preventive strategy because implementation of the policies by all staff members keeps major issues from developing. When a staff member ignores building rules or otherwise shows a lack of support for school policies, it is ultimately the principal's responsibility to let him or her know that such behavior is not an option.

Staff Visibility

When students do not see staff members, the likelihood of rule violations occurring increases dramatically. At a minimum, staff members should be visible to students before school, after school, and during passing periods, recesses, lunch, bus loading and unloading, and assemblies.

As staff members develop a buildingwide discipline plan, they should determine if there are any locations or times of the day when their visibility is lacking. One way to do this is to analyze discipline data to see where and when infractions occur and then develop a plan to deal with the high-incident areas. An example may be that 90 percent of the discipline referrals happen during lunchtime in the northwest athletic field. If it is determined that staff visibility or supervision is a concern in this area, action should be taken to increase staff presence in the athletic field.

Sunnyside High School also developed a rubric to assess staff visibility. This rubric is used by individual staff members to determine how well they enact the building policies regarding staff visibility and supervision. We have adapted this rubric in Figure 6.4.

FIGURE 6.4

STAFF VISIBILITY RUBRIC

Standing in the Hallway During Passing Period	5 In between every class	4 75% of the time	3 50% of the time	2 25% of the time	1 What hallway?
Attending School Functions (Assemblies)	5 In assigned area with class during every event	4 At the event, in general assigned area	3 At the event, random placement	2 Attend some events	1 Not at events

Variations to the left of the dotted line are ideal.
Variations to the left of the solid line are acceptable.
Variations to the right of the solid line are unacceptable.

In addition, Sunnyside High School decided as a staff to develop a reward system for staff supervision of students in which the principal randomly passes out raffle tickets to staff members seen supervising students in the hallways. This is followed by a drawing at each weekly staff meeting. The first week of the month, the teacher whose name is drawn receives a free lunch. The second week, the teacher drawn has a class covered by an administrator. The third week results in another free lunch. The fourth week's winner gets his or her car detailed, washed, and waxed by the auto detailing class at the high school. This has been a very popular technique that has resulted in significantly increased staff supervision in the halls.

Parent Communication

Parent communication regarding enforcement of building issues is critical. Zehm and Kottler (1993) believe that parents can be our greatest allies and can make our jobs much easier. Marzano (2003) states that communication with parents can be used as both a negative and a positive consequence of student behaviors.

Every effort should be made to keep parents updated and informed when it comes to the buildingwide discipline plan. This helps develop a common level of expectations and partnership with the parents, and it also increases the likelihood of preventing discipline problems from occurring.

Just as you contact parents regarding the enforcement of classroom discipline policies, you should also contact parents when students violate buildingwide discipline policies. Usually the principal or assistant principal does this after an office referral. The building policy regarding communication, whatever it is, should be clear to all staff members so that communication is not neglected.

It is important for parents to realize that discipline will be maintained on a buildingwide basis as well as on a classroom basis. At the beginning of the year, the principal should send home a bulletin reviewing the building rules and the system of consequences. Sending home the building rules communicates to every parent that discipline is a high priority on both levels. Some schools require that parents sign a form indicating that they have read the rules and support the consequences. This gives the added emphasis needed to form a strong parent-school partnership.

Parent communication should not cease when students graduate to secondary schools. In fact, in many cases, it is more important than ever to have strong communications with secondary school parents. Thompson (1998) warns teachers not to underestimate the importance of working with parents and reminds us that parents of secondary school students are as concerned about their children's education as are parents of younger children.

Compliance with Instructions from All Staff

A building rule that must be communicated to every student is that anyone who is a building employee is to be obeyed at all times. This includes administrators, teachers, para-educators, secretaries, custodians, and cooks. Students need to understand that they are to follow every staff member's instructions and that, while it is okay to disagree, it is not an option to disobey. When students clearly understand this as a building policy, it helps prevent discipline problems, because the circle of adults responsible for monitoring student behavior increases.

"It Takes a Village" Approach

It is critically important for all staff members to remember that any time they see any student violating a building rule, they are to intervene immediately. Staff members should have the philosophy that "every student is my student." The grade level or subject a staff member teaches should never be a factor when supporting buildingwide discipline policies. Once again, this widens the circle of adults monitoring student behaviors.

Communicating and Teaching the Building Rules

Just as is the case with classroom rules, the building rules should be clear and should be taught to the students. This should be done the first week of school. Also, the rules should be retaught anytime students demonstrate that they do not understand or are not following the building rules.

Prior to the start of the school year, teachers should be given a list of building rules that need to be taught to students the first week of school. The principal should stop by all classrooms or hold an assembly to discuss and teach the building rules to all students.

Rules and procedures for specific areas of the building should also be taught. An effective strategy is to hold a practice assembly the first week of school to review the assembly entrance, exit, and behavior policies. Students should be taken to the lunchroom the first week of school to review the lunchroom procedures, including entering and exiting procedures. Bus loading and unloading rules should also be thoroughly taught the first week of school. Elementary students should be taken to the playground the first week of school to review how to behave on the playground and what to do when going to and returning from recess.

Citizenship and Academic Recognition Programs

Most schools do an excellent job of recognizing students' outstanding athletic accomplishments during pep assemblies. Students also need to be recognized for outstanding academic and citizenship accomplishments. Just as there should be buildingwide discipline approaches in place, there should be buildingwide student recognition programs in place. This helps emphasize for parents, staff, and students that academics and citizenship are highly valued.

The most powerful recognition programs are specific. Citizenship awards that state exactly what a student did are more meaningful than general awards. Examples of specific awards are "improving from a *B* to an *A*" or "reporting building graffiti." Recognition programs are not only a great public relations strategy; they also help prevent discipline problems as students become motivated to demonstrate good behavior.

Buildingwide Pride

Pride is another powerful motivator that should be reinforced in schools. Many schools work hard to foster a level of positive pride that is felt throughout the building. The reason for this is that pride has a direct impact on students' behavior. As students develop pride, pride creates a particular identity, and it is the nature of that identity that drives future behaviors.

If students feel a positive pride—pride in good behavior—they will want to do well. If, however, the pride is negative—that is, they take pride in being "the worst"—it will have a negative impact on student behaviors. Pride can be a school's best friend or its worst enemy. The implication is that schools must not let pride develop unguided but must instead make a focused effort to develop the positive aspects of pride.

Staff members should do everything possible to foster positive pride. Displaying student work, advertising accomplishments, complimenting the student body, and keeping the building clean and aesthetically appealing are just some of the approaches that can be used to achieve this goal.

Rules off of School Grounds

It is important for students to know that school policies apply on the way to and from school, even if they are not on school grounds. Administrators and teachers need to communicate that school policies are in effect from the moment a student leaves his or her home in the morning until he or she returns from school at the end of the day. While it is difficult to provide the supervision over a large area, administrators and other personnel should periodically walk and drive around the school grounds before and after school. A very effective approach is for the principal to drive by specific bus stops in the morning. If students are caught smoking, fighting, or breaking other rules, the consequences should be the same as if the students were at school.

Building Blind Spots

A building blind spot is any area of the building where it is difficult to observe students. By their very nature, building blind spots have a low degree of staff visibility. Because students realize that staff members cannot easily see them in these locations, the likelihood of fights and other serious rule violations in these locations is high. There are two types of blind spots: those created because of poor building design, and those that result from a lack of staff visibility.

Staff should formally examine all locations of their building to identify blind spots. Next, they should take steps to maximize staff visibility in these locations. Setting up duty rosters and setting clear expectations for staff supervision are ways the administration can deal with the problem proactively.

Angry Parents

The ability to deal effectively with angry parents is an important skill that can prevent bigger discipline issues from arising. When you work with angry parents to help them resolve their concerns, strong relationships are developed, making it more likely that those parents will support you in the future.

It is inevitable that you will be faced with angry parents at some point in your career. Many times they are upset over issues that are misunderstood or based on misinformation. When faced with these situations, you can calm a parent down and help him or her become supportive of you and the school if you remain composed and do the following:

- Start the conference with positive statements about the student.
- Let the parent vent.
- Remain calm, and don't get defensive.
- Maintain eye contact.
- Communicate you are listening (e.g., take notes).
- Let the parent get to his or her agenda first.
- Discuss the future (i.e., don't get hung up on the past).
- End abusive conferences gracefully and swiftly.
- Admit mistakes.

Dealing with angry parents is one of the most difficult skills to develop. It takes time, maturity, and practice, yet once it is mastered it is one of the most valuable skills you can have as a teacher. However, there will always be some parents who, no matter how skilled you are, will not be pacified, due to other issues that are beyond your control. In these situations, involve your administrator, the school counselor, or other school support staff.

These are some of the strategies that can be used by all staff to prevent discipline problems from occurring on a buildingwide basis. The next chapter deals with consequences that should be developed systemically for use when prevention is not enough.

7

Buildingwide Consequences

Just as it is in the classroom, the major focus of buildingwide discipline should be a preventive approach to rule violations and student disruptions. Staffs must remember, however, that no matter how many preventive approaches they take to maintain an effective buildingwide discipline system, there will also be a need for an effective system of buildingwide consequences.

Figure 7.1 illustrates the amount of emphasis we believe should be placed on buildingwide consequences versus preventive approaches. This figure is consistent with what we described in Section 1 and illustrated in Figure S1 when we explained the French and Raven (1960) power base model and our belief about the relationship between the power bases of educators in working with students. The preventive approaches of fostering positive teacher-student relationships, clearly defining parameters of acceptable student behaviors, and developing monitoring strategies should be the largest portion of your buildingwide discipline plan.

While there are many reasons building staffs should concentrate on preventive approaches, one of the most important reasons is to limit the need to rely on consequences to student misbehavior. Negative consequences are often ineffective if overused, and dealing them out can be the most disheartening part of the staff's job. Also, the likelihood of staff members becoming frustrated when punishing misbehavior increases significantly, which can cause them to act in ways that will hurt their relations with students and parents. Finally, consequences focus on the negative rather than on the positive.

FIGURE 7.1

BUILDINGWIDE CONSEQUENCES

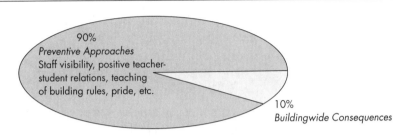

There are reasons why negative consequences may not be effective. One is that schools often do not have a variety of disciplinary actions to choose from, and they therefore overuse the same ones, thereby possibly reducing their impact. A second reason is that only weak or meaningless consequences may be available. Third, staffs often fail to involve parents, thereby lessening the effect of the disciplinary action. Finally, when there is a significant time delay between a rule violation and its consequence, the consequence loses relevance and the end result is made less powerful.

Ideally, the administration and staff should work together to set up a number of building support systems that enable school staff members to select from a range of disciplinary actions in response to student misconduct. This chapter reviews some of the most effective measures: processing, lunch detention, after-school detention and Friday school, office referrals, and in-school suspension. We describe how the consequences are put in place, list their benefits and drawbacks, and identify criteria for effective implementation. Remember that consequences must be related to infractions in a clear way and be consistently and fairly implemented.

Processing

Processing is the practice of sending a student out of the classroom for a time to reflect on his or her actions and make a plan for better choices in the future. Marzano (2003) terms this approach the "written self-analysis" (p. 84). In this approach, students analyze how they feel they contributed to the conflict, how they feel others contributed, how they believe it should be resolved, how they can stop it from happening again, and their final agreement relative to the incident.

Benefits

- Immediate and easily implemented
- A powerful warning
- Gives the student a chance to calm down
- Often prevents the need for an office referral

Drawbacks

- The receiving teacher must monitor the processed student.
- A processing form must be used that meets the student's needs.
- The processing form must be checked.

Criteria for Effective Implementation

- Receiving teachers must accept students when they arrive.
- There must be a place for students to sit.
- There must be an effective consequence for those students who fail to go to processing or who disrupt the processing room.
- Staff must work together to set up the processing system and clearly identify which infractions should result in processing.

Often there is more than one processing form used in a building to meet the needs of the students. For example, variations for different grade levels, special needs students, and students who don't speak English should be considered. Figure 7.2 is an example of one processing form used at a middle school.

Lunch Detention

Lunch detention is the practice of removing students from regular lunch activities to a detention room, where they eat with other students who also have lunch detention. A sack lunch should be provided so that the students who have detention do not have the opportunity to stand in line in the lunchroom and visit when they should be paying the consequence for their poor choices. Some elementary schools have recess detention instead of lunch detention, where students stay in a detention room rather than going to recess.

FIGURE 7.2

PROCESSING FORM

Name: _____Date: _____

Time sent back to class: _____

How many times have you been processed this week? _____

What time is it now? _____

What did you do?

_____

Why did you make this decision?

_____ I wanted attention from others.

_____ I wanted to be in control of the situation.

_____ I wanted to challenge the teacher's authority.

_____ I wanted to avoid doing my schoolwork.

_____ I don't know what I'm supposed to be doing.

_____ I wanted revenge.

_____ I was not prepared for class.

Other: _____

How did your behavior affect you? _____

How did your behavior affect the teacher and the other students?

_____

Why is this kind of behavior unacceptable?

_____

Name two things you are going to do to improve your behavior:

_____

If you go back to the classroom and your behavior continues to be disruptive, what consequences should you receive?

_____

Benefits

- A powerful consequence
- Immediate and easily implemented
- Doesn't require the principal's approval
- An excellent consequence for minor issues

Drawbacks

- Teachers could abuse the practice if not closely monitored.
- It takes some effort to set up on a schoolwide basis.
- It requires adult supervision.

Criteria for Effective Implementation

- Provide a sack lunch so that students don't get to wait in the lunch line.
- Do not allow talking or movement during detention.
- Have stronger consequences, such as after-school detention or Friday school, for students who misbehave.
- Have a system in place that makes skipping detention impossible (e.g., walking students to detention keeps them from skipping).

Give a form to the cook listing who has lunch detention so that the cook can prepare sack lunches for them. Give the same form to the teacher of the last class before lunch so that he or she can walk the appropriate students to detention. If a student earns detention in the afternoon, it can be served the next day. The key is to take the students directly to the detention room from the classroom so that they do not have an opportunity to interact with other students and miss part of their detention.

Coverage for lunch detention can be done in a number of ways. One is to use the principal, vice principal, teachers, and paraprofessionals as supervisors on a rotation system. It is such an important and effective intervention that priority should be placed on devising a way to make it work.

Figure 7.3 is an example of a form that can be used for referring students to lunch detention.

FIGURE 7.3

LUNCH DETENTION FORM

Date: _____   Room #: ____

Teacher Taking Students to Lunch	Buying Lunch?	Completed by Cooks	Referred by	Reason for Referral•
	Yes/No	Paid/Owe		
Teacher 1				
Teacher 2				
Teacher 3				
Teacher 4				
Teacher 5				
Teacher 6				

Reason for Referral: NS = No (Gym) Suit; LD = Lunch Disturbance; CD = Classroom Disturbance; HD = Hallway Disturbance; T = Tardy; G = Gum; AB = Absent; O = Other

After-School Detention and Friday School

Two other schoolwide consequences that are very effective are after-school detention and Friday school. After-school detention is detention that typically lasts for 45 minutes after school. Friday school is used for particularly serious rule violations and typically lasts for two to three hours after school on Fridays. These interventions are usually instituted as more severe consequences than lunch or recess detention. There is nothing magical about Friday, except that Friday school is especially unpopular with students as it is the beginning of the weekend.

Benefits

- Very powerful interventions because students want to go home after school
- Get the parents' attention because they need to give permission and pick up the students
- Used for serious issues
- Immediate

Drawbacks

- Parent contact and permission is required.
- Staff coverage is needed.
- Students will try to skip if transition is not closely monitored.

Criteria for Effective Implementation

- Have a more serious consequence, such as suspension, for students who skip or misbehave.
- Allow no talking or unnecessary movement.
- Require parent permission.
- Have clear criteria regarding which infractions warrant these interventions.
- Have a system that makes skipping impossible (i.e., require teachers to walk students to the detention room and use a detention form to record attendance).

There are creative ways to deal with the drawbacks to these systems. Some schools pay teachers to cover these detentions. Having a secretary monitor the paperwork and be responsible for getting the paperwork to the teachers helps solve the problem of students skipping detention. When parents cannot or will not provide transportation, one option is to substitute three lunch detentions for an after-school detention. Also, it is not necessary to require students to work during this time, but it is necessary that they be quiet. These interventions are so powerful and important to have on the school's list of consequences that it is worth the investment of time and creativity to come up with solutions to any obstacles to implementation.

Figure 7.4 is an example of a form that can be used by staff to refer students to after-school detention and Friday school.

Sunnyside High School in Sunnyside, Washington, has implemented both after-school detention and Friday school as part of their overall school discipline plan. The following figures are forms that have been adapted from their plan for standard operating procedures for detention (Figure 7.5), behaviors that warrant Friday school (Figure 7.6), and standard operating procedures for Friday school (Figure 7.7).

FIGURE 7.4

AFTER-SCHOOL DETENTION AND FRIDAY SCHOOL FORM

Date: _____ Detention Room Teacher: _____
Rm. #: _____ Grade: 6 / 7 / 8

Students	6th Period Teacher Who Will Escort Students to Detention Room	Room #	Referred by	Parent Contact?	Present?

FIGURE 7.5

STANDARD OPERATING PROCEDURES FOR DETENTION

1. An administrator or designee will review the list of students who have been assigned detention.
2. Notification on bright orange paper will be hand-delivered to the teacher by an office assistant at the beginning of 6th period.
3. Teachers will communicate to the students that their detentions must be served that day.
4. Students will remain seated after the final bell has rung and wait to be escorted to the detention room.
5. At the end of the school day, the 6th period teacher will escort the students to detention.
6. Teachers will give the orange papers to the detention supervisor.
7. Students will sign in with the supervisor.
8. If all students listed on the orange paper are absent, the supervisor will turn in the list to the detention office.

FIGURE 7.6

BEHAVIORS THAT WARRANT FRIDAY SCHOOL

When writing referrals for students, teachers will include documentation of the pattern of misbehavior. Please remember that this discipline option will be used for specific, recurring misbehaviors:

- Skipping detention (1st and 2nd offenses)
- 6–8 unexcused tardies
- Recurring discipline issues (a pattern of a particular offense in the moderate category)
- First-time severe offenses that do not warrant out-of-school suspensions, including truancies

FIGURE 7.7

STANDARD OPERATING PROCEDURES FOR FRIDAY SCHOOL

1. An administrator or designee will determine which students must attend Friday school.
2. Notification on bright orange paper will be hand-delivered to the teacher by an office assistant at the beginning of 6th period on Friday.
3. Teachers will communicate to the students that they have Friday school that must be served that day. Students will remain seated after the final bell has rung and wait to be walked down to the detention/Friday school room.
4. At the end of the school day, the teacher will walk the students to the detention/Friday school room.
5. Teachers will give the orange papers to the detention/Friday school supervisor.
6. Students will sign in with the supervisor.
7. If all students listed on the orange paper are absent, the supervisor will turn in the list to the office.

Office Referrals

An effective office referral system has a critical impact on the overall buildingwide discipline system. Office referrals are often "cries for help" that must be taken seriously. They should be used for the most serious and visible issues. If the consequences students receive when they are sent to the office are meaningless, students will not care about an office referral and the number of most serious rule violations will increase. This will undercut the entire buildingwide discipline system.

Benefits

- Immediately removes disruptive students from the classroom
- Gets the attention of parents
- Adds power to a teacher's directives

Drawbacks

- Potential for abuse by some teachers
- Can have a negative impact on office atmosphere
- Administrators may be unavailable

There are ways to ameliorate the drawbacks to office referrals. To prevent teachers with weak classroom management skills from referring students to the office too frequently, make sure that the criteria for such referrals are clearly communicated. If too many students are lining up in the office for too long a period of time, thereby making the office an unpleasant place to be for both students and administrators, work to deal promptly with referrals. And there should be a system in place for taking care of referrals in the principal's absence, such as putting a teacher in charge or contacting a principal from another school regarding difficult situations.

Overreferrals can be avoided by having the principal closely monitor all referrals and work with ineffective teachers to improve their classroom management skills. Because of the potential power of office referrals, it is critical to make certain that the system is working well and that problems are addressed. The important thing is to proactively solve potential problems so that the office referral system is strong and effective.

Criteria for Effective Implementation

Use office referrals for serious infractions, such as cumulative violations, violence, insubordination, gang activity, and sexual harassment.

There are several keys to implementing an effective office referral system. First of all, there must be an excellent communication system in place. Communication begins with the teacher's making a personal contact with the principal about a student's disruptive behavior. The principal determines the consequence for the misbehavior and contacts the parent. After the parent contact, the principal contacts the referring teacher and summarizes the intervention. Finally, if the student has more than one teacher, all the student's teachers receive an e-mail summary of the referral. This helps other teachers support the referring teacher and also gives them information they may need when they are working with the student.

The second key to an effective office referral system is that students who are referred to the office receive immediate and meaningful consequences. Lunch detention and processing usually are not severe enough consequences if an office referral is made appropriately, as teachers have access to these interventions and should use them before sending students to the office. In most instances, an appropriate office referral warrants, at a minimum, parent contact and after-school detention assigned by the principal. Additionally, the student should be addressed as soon as possible.

The third key to an effective office referral system is that staff members must not refer students to the office for issues they should handle themselves. In order to ensure this, staff inservice programs, reviewing what appropriate referrals are and are not and how staff members can deal with minor student infractions themselves, are necessary on a regular basis.

The fourth key is that the office must not be a holding area for students. Students should remain separated and quiet while waiting in the office, and administrators need to consider office referrals a top priority. When it is impossible for an administrator to deal with a student within a reasonable time period, a back-up system should be in place, such as using a buddy room or time-out room until the administrator is available.

Teachers want a student who is referred to the office to receive a powerful and immediate consequence. Most teachers don't mind having the student return to their classrooms after he or she is disciplined, but prior to sending the student back to class it is critically important for the principal to contact the teacher to let him or her know what the consequence was and to ask if it would be appropriate to send the student back to class. When this communication occurs, it completes the cycle of an effective office referral and makes for good staff relations.

In-School Suspension

A powerful and immediate consequence to use with students who are referred for a serious offense is suspension. When out-of-school suspension cannot be implemented, an alternative is in-school suspension. In-school suspension involves keeping the student in an isolated area in the school for a significant period of the day or for one or more days as an alternative to out-of-school suspension. There are several benefits and drawbacks to in-school suspension.

Benefits

- Immediate
- Doesn't require parents to be available
- Removes the student from school activities and visibility
- Ensures the student is monitored by school staff

Drawbacks

- Requires staff supervision
- Requires a private location
- Doesn't always get parents' attention as much as out-of-school suspension does

Criteria for Effective Implementation

- Use sparingly.
- Establish clear criteria for in-school versus out-of-school suspension.
- Have a viable location.
- Assign work to the student.

If in-school suspension is to be one of the interventions used in a school, there are several guidelines that should be followed in setting it up. First of all, it should be used sparingly and there should be clear criteria regarding when a student is given in-school suspension rather than out-of-school suspension. For example, if the principal determines that the parent is supportive but unable to leave work or have the student supervised at home, he or she may decide to assign in-school suspension. Another guideline is that an appropriate location or locations must be available. Some schools actually have an open classroom or storage room that is converted into an in-school suspension room. In other schools, smaller areas are used, such as a corner of the library or of the office with a study carrel for the student to sit and work in.

Staff must be available to supervise in-school suspension. If a separate room is used, this means a staff member must be released from other duties or able to do other duties while supervising in-school suspension. If a study carrel is used, the student must be able to sit and work with minimal staff supervision, as staff who are supervising, such as the librarian or an office staff member, may also be performing other duties. Finally, if in-school suspension is used, it is most effective if teachers assign work for the student to do while serving. Ultimately, as it is the principal or the assistant principal who assigns out-of-school or in-school suspension, it is the principal's responsibility to make sure that the guidelines are followed so that in-school suspension does not become a disrupting factor to other school activities and responsibilities while meeting the needs of the student and the parents.

There are many effective buildingwide consequences that can be put in place as part of a strong overall buildingwide discipline plan. To do it successfully, staff must work together to plan and implement the consequence components.

8

Policies for Specific Building Locations

Certain building locations and events can create difficulties with discipline if not structured and supervised appropriately. Marzano (2003) states that "ecological interventions" should be considered for counteracting "negative consequences of the school's physical characteristics or of the school's schedule" (p. 107). Assemblies, hallways, the school office, the lunchroom, dress code, gangs, and fighting are just some of the areas and events that are often a major source of office referrals and student disturbances. How these are handled sets a buildingwide atmosphere that can be either positive and structured or disruptive and chaotic.

Assemblies

Building assemblies can be an easy and effective way to recognize staff and students, build school pride, and provide information to the entire study body. However, if not structured appropriately, assemblies can create safety and disciplinary problems. Also, assemblies can inspire a strong temptation for students to act inappropriately, such as booing, throwing things, and moving to different locations. Some schools have actually discontinued assemblies because of the problems they caused.

A great way to start addressing the challenges posed by assemblies is to create and communicate an assembly seating chart indicating where each class is to sit. Classes should come in quietly and go directly to their assigned seats, ready to listen and watch during the assembly. Figure 8.1 is an example of an assembly seating chart for a typical elementary school.

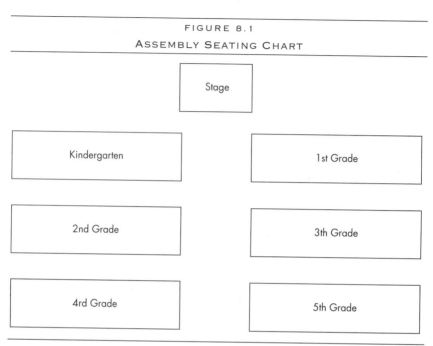

FIGURE 8.1
ASSEMBLY SEATING CHART

Building staff should decide what behaviors are acceptable during assemblies and formally teach those behaviors to all students. It is recommended that buildings actually have a practice assembly at the beginning of the year to teach expectations and have the students demonstrate their understanding of appropriate assembly behaviors.

As we review specific expectations in this section, consider the developmental age and grade level of your students as you determine which should apply to your school. You may alter expectations accordingly, by allowing high school students more freedom, for example, as they have earned it with their added maturity. It is important for staff to analyze the specific needs of their students as they assess their buildingwide discipline system and make adjustments accordingly.

Entering and exiting the stands in an assembly can be the most disruptive part of an assembly and can also create a safety issue if not done correctly. It is advisable to require students entering the stands to go to the top and move over rather than haphazardly charging up the stands and running to select their seats. This process helps to ensure an orderly and safe student entrance. Likewise, a safe and structured exiting process can be instituted by beginning with the top row and requiring each row to stand, move to the center, and then exit (see Figures 8.2 and 8.3).

FIGURE 8.2

ENTERING PROCEDURE FOR ASSEMBLIES

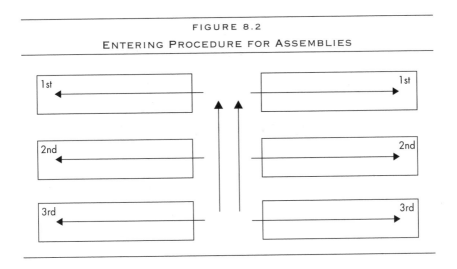

FIGURE 8.3

EXITING PROCEDURE FOR ASSEMBLIES

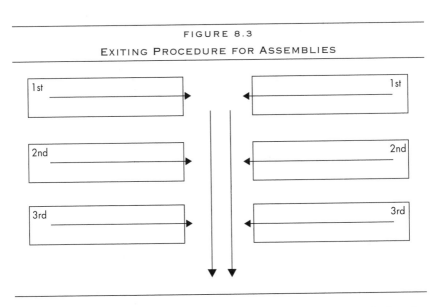

It is critical that teachers actually sit with their students during the assemblies. As is the case in the classroom, there is no substitute for teachers being near their students to ensure good behavior. It is also an excellent idea to have a detention room during assemblies. Students whose behaviors have been disruptive can stay in the supervised detention room rather than attend the assembly. In addition, students who misbehave during assemblies can be sent to the detention room.

In high school, there may be an alternative room made available to students during assemblies. This is a supervised room in which students may read or work on their schoolwork rather than attending the assembly. This should be available only during optional assemblies.

Many times, when students are allowed to leave an assembly alone, they wander the building and do not return to their classroom. It is recommended that students not be allowed to leave an assembly alone and that they return to their classrooms with the teachers who brought them to the assembly. Figure 8.4 gives an example of assembly rules that a building staff may adopt.

FIGURE 8.4

ASSEMBLY RULES

1. Students are to show their appreciation during assemblies by cheering and clapping. Booing, hooting, and yelling are not acceptable assembly behaviors.
2. Items are never to be thrown during assemblies.
3. Students are to walk with their teacher to assemblies. After entering the gym, students are to wait for their teacher's signal before going into the stands. Students are to sit with their teacher in the stands during assemblies.
4. Students are to use the restrooms prior to assemblies.
5. As soon as the assembly begins, all students are to be quiet and give the speaker their undivided attention.
6. At the conclusion of the assembly, students will be dismissed one row at a time. The back row will always be dismissed first. When a row is dismissed, students are to walk to the center of the stands and exit to the gym floor.
7. Students are to remain with their teacher when transitioning to the gym, sitting in the stands, and exiting the gym.
8. Students are to return to their classroom with the teacher who brought them to the gym.

Some schools set up a reward system to reinforce positive assembly behavior. An example of such a system is that each teacher picks the student with the best behavior during the assembly and asks him or her to report to the office for a treat. This is most appropriate at the elementary level.

Lunchrooms

Many schools experience more student disruptions and discipline issues in their lunchrooms than any other building location or activity other than recess. If structured inappropriately, the lunchroom can create a great number of behavior problems.

There are many reasons why students tend to act inappropriately during lunch. One is that lunchrooms usually have only one or two supervisors for hundreds of students. Students also tend to look at lunchtime as an opportunity to socialize and unwind. If rules have not been taught and supervision is minimal, there is a real potential for disruptive behaviors. Each school staff should determine the lunch rules and policies that are important for their school. The students should then be taught the appropriate lunchroom behaviors. In addition, every effort should be made to maximize the number of lunchroom supervisors, and these supervisors should continually move throughout their assigned areas while they are on duty.

One way to keep the lunchroom organized and structured is to require students to first take their seats and listen to announcements and instructions, as opposed to immediately lining up to get their lunches. Students are much easier to supervise while they are seated. Allowing only a certain number of students to line up at a time will also help maintain structure and order. Allowing only students who are acting appropriately to line up further reinforces the behavior that is expected.

When it is time to leave the lunchroom, students should be dismissed by the lunchroom supervisors. Again, dismissing students only when they are demonstrating appropriate behaviors reinforces what is expected. A system that allows all the students to get up and leave as soon as the bell rings invites disruption and chaos. Some schools require students to wash their tables and pick up their own garbage before being dismissed. The rationale for this approach is based on the belief that this is a good life skill and that students should be responsible for their own messes.

Figure 8.5 gives an example of lunchroom rules that a school may adopt.

FIGURE 8.5

LUNCH RULES

1. Students should use the restrooms, phones, and vending machines prior to entering the lunchroom.
2. Students are not allowed to leave the lunchroom until they are excused by a supervisor.
3. Prior to being dismissed, students must wipe off their tables with the wet rags that are located in the lunchroom.
4. Students are to be escorted to and from the lunchroom by their teacher.

Hallways

In many schools, there are a number of rule violations and inappropriate behaviors occurring in the hallways during passing periods. Typically, passing in the hallways involves the movement of a large number of students with a minimal amount of staff supervision. This results in the increased likelihood of pushing, running, and fighting. Also, when students are disruptive in the hallways, they often bring the disruptive behavior with them into the classroom.

There are strategies that can be employed to ensure structured passing periods. Maximizing staff visibility is the most important. Having teachers simply stand by their classroom doors while students are changing classes, simultaneously monitoring the students entering their rooms and watching those in the hallway, greatly increases staff visibility and helps put students on their best behavior. In addition, principals should communicate the expectation that staff should not only be visible during passing periods but also must do their part by being a physical presence in the hallways. This sets a model for staff to follow, as well as allows the principal to see which teachers are monitoring the hallways.

Teaching students what the hallway expectations are is another important strategy. How do you want students moving between classrooms? Do you want them to walk or run? Do you expect them to walk in lines, or is it all right for them to walk with their friends, quietly and respectfully, between class periods?

Outlining immediate and meaningful consequences for inappropriate hallway behavior is also very important. Just like in the classroom, students need to understand that if they break the rules, there will be consequences as a result of the infraction. All staff members should be encouraged to implement consequences on a consistent basis for inappropriate hallway behavior. If the rules apply only with some teachers, students quickly learn which teachers will let them stretch the rules.

> **Tip Box**
>
> *Formula to avoid hall problems:* Appropriate levels of staff visibility + hallway passing policies that are taught + consequences that are consistently enforced by all staff.

Recesses and Intramural Sports

Recesses and intramural sports are another typical source of student disruptions and rule violations. Often the number of staff supervisors during such activities is limited. Also, since large numbers of students are quite active during these times, the likelihood of discipline issues arising is quite high.

There are ways to establish a structured and orderly environment during recesses. First of all, staff must agree on recess policies and procedures and review them at least annually, just as they do with buildingwide discipline policies. Second, staff must teach the policies and procedures to the students and enforce structured exiting and entering procedures. The ways students leave the building on the way to recess and enter the building after recess are critical in terms of setting the stage for appropriate behaviors. When rules are taught, entrance and exit procedures should also be taught. Using a detention room for rule violations is important because it makes an immediate and effective consequence for disruptive behavior available to recess supervisors.

Recess supervisors must be supported. Students must be taught that they are to follow the supervisor's instructions at all times, and the supervisor should have an effective way of communicating with teachers and the administration when students do not comply with the rules. Forms that can be quickly filled out by the recess supervisor can be used to keep other staff informed when the students act inappropriately during recess. Figure 8.6 is an example of such a recess referral form.

FIGURE 8.6

RECESS REFERRAL FORM

Student: _____ Date: _____

Violation:
___ Noncompliance
___ Shoving
___ Harassment
___ Not stopping when bell rang
___ Disrupting games
___ Other: _____

Consequence:
___ Warned
___ Detention
___ Other: _____

Copies: Administration   Teacher   Counselor

If at all possible, walkie-talkies or some other type of communication equipment should be made available to the recess supervisors so that they can get help quickly if necessary.

A critical component of communication and support for recess supervisors is for the administration to meet with them on a regular basis to monitor how things are going and to address issues as they arise. Weekly or monthly meetings with the recess supervisors are a critical component of the support system.

> **Tip Box**
>
> *Formula to avoid problems during recesses and intramural sports:* Teach the required behaviors + have the appropriate number of supervisors + implement immediate and consistent consequences for rule violations.

Figure 8.7 is an example of some rules that can be used during recess or noontime intramural sports. The language can be adjusted depending on the activity to which the rules apply.

Student Restrooms

Student restrooms can become an area of concern due to the fact that adults are seldom, if ever, in these areas. Jones (1987) states that if adults

---

FIGURE 8.7

RULES FOR STUDENTS PARTICIPATING
IN NOON INTRAMURAL SPORTS

1. Students must be dismissed by a supervising staff member before going to intramural sports.
2. Students are to return all equipment to the appropriate locations at the conclusion of intramural sports.
3. At the conclusion of intramural sports, students are to go to the designated areas.
4. Students are to wait in the designated areas until directed to enter the building.
5. After entering the building, students are to walk in a quiet and organized manner to their classrooms.

---

stay out of student restrooms, the restrooms belong to the students and then become areas where major problems occur.

There are several things that a school staff should do to keep the restroom problems to a minimum. If the school is still in the design stage, the sinks should be placed in the halls rather than in the restrooms. This keeps the amount of time that students are out of the visual field of adults to a minimum.

In most situations, you won't have the luxury of designing the restrooms. In that case, it is important to set up a monitoring system. Students usually go to the restrooms alone, so staff members should periodically drop by student restrooms unannounced to monitor student behavior. Administrators should make this part of their daily walk through the building.

Buildingwide, especially at the elementary level, there should be a policy that no more than one student be excused to go to the restroom at a time to diminish the possibility of restroom problems. The exception to this rule would be special conditions that have been set up for a particular student, such as a buddy system on a contract for a student who needs at least student monitoring. Using a restroom pass helps facilitate this policy. Keeping a written record of which student goes to the restroom at what time helps to pinpoint who may have been involved in a restroom incident when the approximate time of the incident is known. Figure 8.8 is an example of a restroom chart.

The expectation that there be no litter in the restrooms, just as throughout the rest of the school, should be clearly communicated to students. Student restrooms are often the worst area of the school in regard to accumulation of litter. One way of encouraging good student behavior and

FIGURE 8.8
RESTROOM CHART

Name	Time Left for Restroom	Time Returned
_____	_____	_____
_____	_____	_____
_____	_____	_____
_____	_____	_____
_____	_____	_____

preventing litter in restrooms is to periodically give rewards, such as cans of pop, extra recess, or popcorn, to classrooms whose student restroom has had the best restroom record for a particular period of time.

Portables

Portables and the grounds around portables can be areas of student misbehavior and problems. Again, the key is to monitor these areas, especially during transition times. Adults need to be visible, as visibility proactively heads off all types of problems. Staff presence is also important before and after school, as kids can "hang out" in these areas and create disciplinary issues. In some districts, video cameras are located so as to monitor for vandalism. When monitoring and supervising is part of the buildingwide discipline plan, numerous problems can be prevented.

Bus Loading and Unloading

It is important that students get on and off school buses in an orderly, respectful fashion. The behaviors they display when loading and unloading buses are often carried onto the bus or into the school. The most important strategy is to have sufficient staff supervision during these times. A duty roster should be established, monitored by the principal, and enforced.

When students arrive in the morning, they should be expected to walk quietly off the buses and to the appropriate location. This process should be monitored by supervisors. At the end of the day, students should wait quietly in lines outside of the buses. It is very important that teachers don't excuse their classes before the bell rings at the end of the day; if they do, a situation arises in which students are unsupervised and accidents and problems can occur. It is also critical from a safety perspective that walking between buses not be allowed. This should be monitored by staff.

Finally, rule violations in regard to loading and unloading buses should be treated just the same as rule violations in the classroom or in any other part of the school. Making this clear to students helps to prevent discipline problems.

Dress Code

Many schools have expectations for student dress even if they don't have school uniforms. This is based on the belief that dressing appropriately affects school and classroom climate and sets the stage for respectful behavior. However, even when a school has a dress code, many staff members look the other way when it comes to compliance with the code. This is an issue that should be closely examined. When there is a dress code in place, it is as important that everyone enforce it as it is that other school rules are consistently enforced.

Enforcing a dress code can be a difficult process. It is not easy to prove to an unsympathetic parent that a student's clothes are causing a disruption to the educational process, especially when the clothes they are wearing are one of the new popular styles. Also, the enforcement of a student dress code often comes down to a subjective interpretation. What is inappropriate to one teacher might be acceptable to another teacher.

If the staff chooses to deal with the dress code issue, there are several steps that should be taken. First of all, a common set of standards should be established and consequences for failure to comply with the standards should be determined. The dress code standards need to be precise and understandable. Second, the dress code policy and its rationale need to be communicated to the parents in newsletters, assemblies, and conferences. Third, the policies and their rationale need to be taught to the students during classroom lessons and school assemblies. Finally, students who violate the dress code need to be dealt with immediately. Some schools make an "all call" in the morning, asking teachers to send all dress code violators to the office. This sends a strong message that the dress code will be enforced immediately each and every day. Parents of violators should be called, and if a student cannot get a change of clothing from his or her home, the office should supply the student with a long shirt to cover the unacceptable clothes. Figure 8.9 is an example of a student dress code.

FIGURE 8.9

STUDENT DRESS CODE

Styles that disrupt the educational process are prohibited.

- Pants, shirts, and blouses must not be revealing.
- Exposed undergarments or midriffs are not acceptable.
- Tank tops and tube tops must be worn with a shirt with sleeves.
- Shorts and skirts must come down to the length of the student's extended fingertips.
- Spandex clothing is permitted in P.E. classes only.
- Sagging pants, hanging chains, sunglasses, and clothing that displays profanity; encourages violence or the use of drugs, alcohol, or tobacco; or has sexual connotations are not permitted.

Gang Issues

Gang members are typically involved in violence, harassment, and drugs, and gangs often get their members from students in schools. Gangs have absolutely no place in schools. Immediate intervention is the only appropriate response to any sign of gang activity. There are many examples of schools that have not responded quickly or powerfully enough to signs of gang activity. Once gangs are allowed to get a foothold in the schools, it becomes very difficult to undo the damage they have caused.

Many schools claim they have a no-tolerance policy for any type of gang activity. However, when signs of gangs surface, the schools often don't respond in a rapid and meaningful manner. It is essential that students, staff, and parents know that any sign of gang activity will be met with severe consequences. These typically involve a suspension that stays in effect until there is a meeting with the parents, police, and school personnel.

Staff members periodically should be given inservice training to make them aware of current gang signs and activities. There are certain signs of gang involvement that staff members should watch out for constantly, including gang clothing, gang tattoos, gang language, and gang hand gestures. These often change, so it is important that someone who is knowledgeable about current situations, such as the police, train the staff.

Fighting

There is no place for violence in our schools. Schools need to take steps to be certain parents and students know that a "no tolerance for violence" policy will be strictly enforced. A strong approach is to have a "consequence scale" showing the hierarchy of consequences for different offenses. In this hierarchy, fighting is listed as having a consequence of suspension on the first offense. Figure 8.10 is an example of such a consequence scale.

FIGURE 8.10
CONSEQUENCE SCALE

Rule Violation	Consequence
Minor disruption	Processing
Minor talking out of turn	Processing
Gum chewing	Lunch detention
Tardiness	Lunch detention
Profanity	After-school detention
Noncompliance	After-school detention
Cumulative violations	Friday school
Shoving/pushing	Friday school
Sexual harassment	Friday school
Fighting	Suspension

What the school means by a "no tolerance for violence" policy needs to be clearly communicated to students and parents. Typically, this means that students who hit other students for any reason will be placed on an immediate suspension. The policy must also apply to all situations. Students need to know that they have a right to defend themselves if they are hit, but they do not have the right to start hitting back. Students need to be taught how to defend themselves appropriately. They should be taught that the best way to stop a fight is to go to the nearest staff member or yell for help.

The rationale for this policy is that students need to learn not to turn to violence in an effort to counteract violence. When students start hitting other students who hit them first, it does not stop violence but instead creates bigger fights and more violence. When students retaliate by hitting those who hit them first, the last student standing is not necessarily the student who was initially hit. Some students think it is okay to start hitting a student who hit them first and will look for opportunities to "legally" beat someone up. Students should be taught that when someone breaks a rule about hitting, it is the school's responsibility to punish the offender, not the student's responsibility.

You may wonder what the consequences should be for students who hit a student after being hit themselves. Although the building rule should clearly state that any student who decides to hit another student will be suspended, the student who hits in retaliation should be suspended for a much shorter time period than the person who initiated the attack. Parents need to understand the school's policy about no fighting, even in retaliation. Figure 8.11 is an example of a way to communicate this policy to parents in the form of a letter.

This concludes the section on buildingwide discipline. We hope that the ideas shared are helpful in bringing about a strong system of discipline and a positive climate in your school.

End of Section Reflection Questions

1. What are the components of a buildingwide discipline system?
2. If you were to visit a school for the first time, what would be some immediate indications that the staff has established a structured and orderly buildingwide environment?
3. What impact can a high degree of structure and discipline have on a building's students, staff, and parents?

FIGURE 8.11

PARENT LETTER REGARDING THE SCHOOL'S NO FIGHTING POLICY

Dear Parents:

Parents have the right to expect that their student's school does everything possible to ensure a safe learning environment. In an effort to maintain a safe school climate in which students are free from the threat of violence, we have instituted the following policy.

Our school has a "no tolerance for violence" policy. This simply means that no student will be allowed to resort to fighting or hitting for any reason on the way to school, while at school, on the way home from school, or at any school event. Our policy states that any student who decides to settle a problem by hitting or fighting will immediately be suspended from school. There will be no exceptions to this rule, and it will be discussed with all students the first day of school.

One aspect of the policy that parents need to understand is that the no fighting or hitting rule covers all situations. A student who hits others will be suspended, *even if another student hit him or her first.* Students must realize that it is the staff's responsibility, not the students' responsibility, to discipline a student who hits.

When students believe they have the right to hit somebody who hits them first, they can use it as an excuse to hit students. If a student is ever hit while at school, he or she must find a nonviolent way to react. This includes blocking the student who hits, getting away from the student, and letting a staff member know that the incident occurred. The administration, as well as the staff, will be discussing nonviolent measures that students can take to deal with violence from their peers.

I hope that every parent understands that our no fighting and hitting rules are a crucial part of our effort to maintain a nonviolent school climate. We believe it is illogical to expect students to learn in an atmosphere that is not safe or in which students feel threatened. Thank you in advance for your support.

Sincerely,
School Principal

---

4. Which discipline components are strong in your building?
5. Which components are weak in your building? Specifically, what needs to be changed and how?
6. What building locations need to be addressed?
7. What building policies need to be improved? How?
8. What are the most important concepts of this section?

SECTION 3

CAN'T-MISS DISCIPLINE STRATEGIES

Can't-Miss Discipline Strategies

During our collective 43 years in elementary and secondary school administration, we have made literally thousands of classroom observations. During these observations, we have noticed certain strategies that consistently have a positive impact on student behavior and academic performance. These strategies are powerful and easy to use. Each strategy involves a commonsense approach that most teachers are well aware of but sometimes forget to emphasize.

This section provides summaries of these strategies with the hope that you can find ways to use them in your professional life. Most of the strategies apply to the classroom setting, but some of them have buildingwide application. We have organized this section using the discipline component system that was reviewed earlier, categorizing by relationship strategies, parameter strategies, monitoring strategies, and consequence strategies.

9

Relationship Strategies

We strongly believe that positive relationships form the foundation of a positive discipline plan. In Chapter 1, we built a case for making positive teacher-student relations the largest portion of your discipline plan. In this chapter, we share specific strategies that teachers and other staff members can use to help develop strong relationships with students, which in turn help decrease the number of student discipline incidents. We also share some strategies you can use to develop positive relations with parents. Such relationships help to dramatically increase your positive power over students because the students know that you and their parents are working together rather than being at odds with each other. Below we list 12 strategies and expand on how you can put them to work for you.

Don't Be One of the Kids

There are some teachers who fail to enforce various rules because they want students to like them. This is unprofessional and results in the teacher's losing the respect of both students and staff members. When teachers try to act more like students than teachers, they undermine the buildingwide discipline system and help to create a morale issue throughout the building. Do you have favorites? Do you look the other way with some kids? Not only is this type of behavior a liability to the buildingwide discipline plan; it also negatively affects the building atmosphere. It is important for you to be professional with students and to show clearly by your words and actions that, while you value and care about your students, you are in charge and they must treat you with respect and not as a friend or peer. This should be consistent behavior that you display with all your students.

Never Use Humiliation or Sarcasm

Some teachers think it is all right to use sarcasm because it creates a humorous situation that makes the students laugh. But humor that comes at the expense of a student's dignity is always unwise, unprofessional, and inappropriate. It also sets a dangerous pattern that is often emulated by students. Teachers often have no idea what personal situations a student might be facing, and a student who seems secure enough to handle the sarcasm may be devastated when the sarcasm is coupled with a personal problem the teacher is unaware of.

> **Tip Box**
>
> *The bottom line:* Sarcasm is dangerous, cruel, and unprofessional and should not be used in schools.

Start Parent Conferences with Positive Statements

A major goal for every parent conference is to increase the understanding, communication, respect, and cooperation between the parents and the teacher. When this occurs, the likelihood of the parents and school working together to meet the needs of students increases dramatically.

One of the first messages you should communicate during a parent conference is that you care about their child. When parents realize you appreciate and value their son or daughter, they are more likely to work cooperatively with the school. Remember, parents see their child as a reflection of themselves. Consequently, when you compliment a student, you are also complimenting the parents. There will be time in the meeting to discuss any concerns you have. Starting a conference by complimenting and enumerating the positive aspects of a child in no way limits the opportunity to discuss problems.

Start Difficult Conferences with the Student Outside of the Room

One of the most destructive things to a teacher's authority that a student can witness is an argument between a teacher and a parent. If there is any possibility the conference might not go well, start the meeting with the student outside of the room. After the difficult issues have been settled and a strategy that both you and the parents can support is in place, the student can be asked to join the conference.

Let the Parents Get Their Message Out First

No matter what issue you want to discuss with parents in a conference concerning their child, first listen to what the parents have to say. If you don't, they won't hear anything you have to say. Do everything you can to assure the parents you are listening, including making eye contact, taking notes, nodding your head at appropriate times, paraphrasing main points, and acknowledging their point. If the parents think you don't care about their issues, they won't be as inclined to care about yours.

Make Some Concessions

Whenever possible during a conference, find points that a parent makes that you can agree with or apologize for something that you did that upset the parent. For example, if a father says that you didn't let him know soon enough that the student was struggling, concur, saying, for example, "I probably should have called you sooner." This validates his concern and lets him know that the issue is not to establish blame but to work together to solve the problem.

Talk About the Future

As soon as possible in a parent conference, begin talking about the future, making a plan with parents and students to remedy whatever problem exists rather than getting stuck on the past. For example, if the issue is that a student is not completing his or her homework, establish the problem and then move on to develop a plan regarding how to be sure the homework is completed in the future and how to improve communication between the teacher and the parents regarding any missed work.

Call Parents Before a Disciplined Student Gets Home

When you discipline or correct a student, there is always the possibility the student will give his or her parents a skewed version of what happened. Students typically leave out critical information in an effort to make it appear that they did nothing wrong and were treated unfairly. Often parents buy students' stories and become upset with you. In some situations, the issue festers until a parent angrily contacts the school to deal with you. At this point, you are faced with the difficult task of calming the parent down and presenting the correct facts.

Taking a few minutes to proactively contact a parent before a disciplined student gets home often saves you a headache. This procedure usually prepares the parent for the student's stories and prevents a parent blowup that is based on misinformation. Also, proactive communication is usually appreciated by parents.

There is no question that teachers do a better job of reporting unbiased and factual information to parents than students do. When considering the importance of making a proactive parent contact, ask yourself who you want reporting the "facts" to the parent, the student or you?

Tip Box
Remember: Every student has a PhD in parent manipulation, so be proactive!

Actively Encourage Parents to Call the School

Far too often, parents hear rumors about school incidents that make no sense. Most of the time, this information is inaccurate. When parents do not contact the school to check the stories out, they can form negative opinions about the school or a teacher. In an effort to head off these situations, teachers and administrators should continually urge parents to contact the school any time they have questions or concerns that bother them. When doing so, let the parents know that the school welcomes and appreciates their questions.

School bulletins, parent conferences, and back-to-school events are great opportunities to remind parents that they should not hesitate to interact with building staff. You should also provide parents with building and classroom phone numbers and the best times to call.

Increase the Power of Praise

Being specific when you give praise to students helps to create a positive learning situation because it clearly lets all your students know the type of behaviors and performances you are looking for. General statements of approval, such as "Good job" or "That's great" do not communicate what a student did to warrant them. Nonspecific praise can cause students to think they earned compliments for the wrong reason. An example of specific praise is, "Your writing has improved significantly since you have increased the use of examples and clarified your authorial voice."

Another way to increase the power and impact of praise is to make it personal by simply stating the student's name. Also remember that it is important that your remarks be sincere and justified. Students will react negatively even to positive feedback when it is manipulative and not deserved.

Be careful to consider the age of your students when giving praise. Sprick (1985) states that compliments given to older students in front of their peers can be embarrassing and unwanted. In these cases, you might consider commending the student in a private manner. You can also use an alternative method of praise, such as sending home a letter or rewarding a student with a certificate. With younger students, public approval is often desired and effective. Praise needs to be developmentally appropriate.

Smile and Greet the Students

Wong and Wong (1998) suggest that standing by the door each morning as the students enter the classroom is a great way to let students know not only that you enjoy your job and care about each student, but that you are also actively paying attention to the students and observing their actions. Individually greeting your students as they enter the classroom is an effective strategy for both relationship building and monitoring student behavior.

Learn Students' Names

When you address a student by his or her name, it dignifies the student and communicates two things: "You're important enough for me to know your name" and "You're more than just another student to me." Students are quick to realize that you do not know their names. When you use words like "you" or when you call them by the wrong name, there is a strong likelihood that they will believe you do not respect or value them.

You should take the time to learn students' names as quickly as possible. This can be a difficult process, depending on how many students you have. Techniques for learning students' names include the following:

- Studying the school annual, and put names with faces
- Looking for defining characteristics of each student
- Studying the roster at the end of the day, and visualize each student
- Putting students' pictures in your seating chart

> **Tip Box**
>
> *Note:* It's a good idea to have the students say their names the first time you meet them so that you know how to pronounce each name correctly.

10

Parameter Strategies

Relationships are the foundation of a strong, positive discipline plan. But stopping with the foundation is insufficient; the second component in a strong discipline plan is the establishment and articulation of clearly defined parameters of acceptable student behaviors. In Chapter 2, we addressed why clear parameters are important, what they consist of, how to establish them, and how to teach them to students. In this chapter, we offer some specific strategies that school staff members can use to help sharpen these parameters to proactively decrease disciplinary problems.

Teach the Discipline Plan and Rules of Conduct

Students learn what they are taught. Why must you teach anything? The answer is obvious: If a subject is not taught, students will most likely fail to learn it. This is why you don't just say to your math students, "Know your math facts," and then move on to the next topic. Instead, you formally teach each aspect of every math concept in a step-by-step, planned process. The same instructional procedures should apply to your discipline plan and rules of conduct. Although this strategy was covered in an earlier section (see Chapter 3), we think it is important enough to be mentioned again.

The best time to teach the discipline plan and rules of conduct is at the beginning of the year. You must, however, be prepared to reteach any aspect of the discipline plan or rules of conduct if your students' behavior makes it apparent they have forgotten the rules or are not complying with them. A key time for such reteaching is after a long break or vacation.

Teach and Enforce a Classroom Signal

One of the most important things you can teach your students the first day of school is your signal. Whatever your signal is, when you make it, all students should immediately stop what they are doing and give you their undivided attention. A signal should be used during transition periods, prior to giving students instruction, and any other time you need every student's complete attention.

> ### Tip Box
>
> *Warning:* If you give a signal and continue your instruction before verifying that every student has appropriately responded to the signal, students will soon realize that the signal is not important. Also, if one student is allowed to disobey the signal, other students will begin to ignore it as well.

Get the "Junk" Off the Desks

Paperback books, CD players, dolls, and other items often wind up on desks during classroom instruction. Each of these items is a potential distraction for the student. This distraction can be eliminated by directing students to put all items that are not needed for the lesson in their desks or on the floor.

> ### Tip Box
>
> *Rule of thumb:* If it's not needed for the lesson, it shouldn't be on the desk.

Teach the Logic Behind the Rules

Students, like adults, are more likely to support rules that are logical. Canter and Canter (1997) state that students at intermediate grade levels want to know the reasons for specific rules and how following these rules will help them do better in school. Whereas the logic behind your rules may seem obvious to you, you should not assume that students understand that logic. Students view rules from a different perspective, and what makes sense to you does not always make sense to them. The logic behind some rules, such as bans on gum chewing and hat wearing, truly escapes students. Taking the time to deliberately review rationales for the rules often results in students' being more accepting of them and willing to follow them.

Post Classroom Rules

One of the most common arguments parents and students have against a consequence for misbehavior is that the teacher failed to make the student aware of the rules and consequences. Usually the teacher has communicated this information, but the parent remains skeptical. Posting the rules by the classroom door is an extremely effective way to make certain that there is no question the rules have been communicated to the students on a daily basis. If parents or students claim not to be aware of the rule, you can remind them that the rule not only was taught to the students at the beginning of the year, but also is posted by the door.

Posting the rules is also a reminder to the teacher. Seeing the rules on the wall helps teachers remember the importance of consistently monitoring and enforcing their discipline policies.

Post Building Rules

Buildingwide rules should be posted in locations that are clearly visible to the students every day, such as next to classroom doors. When building rules are posted in areas frequented by both students and staff, including hallways and entrances to common areas in the building, everyone is reminded of the rules and the importance of compliance on a daily basis. An effective procedure to use with parents who claim their child was not aware of a rule is to show them the posted rules and point out that the students see the rules all the time.

Figure 10.1 is an example of a list of buildingwide rules that can be posted in visible locations throughout the school.

Establish a Buildingwide Signal

Some schools use a single signal for the entire building. As the students hear the signal year after year, they become very familiar with it. Substitutes, librarians, and other specialists appreciate the consistency of a buildingwide signal. Also, a buildingwide signal is very helpful during assemblies. Figure 10.2 gives an example of a buildingwide signal and what it means to students.

FIGURE 10.1

BUILDINGWIDE RULES

1. *Violence:* Violence of any type will not be tolerated. Any student who hits someone for any reason (even if he or she was hit first) will be suspended immediately.

2. *Harassment (verbal or physical):* Harassment will result in immediate consequences, including detention, Friday school, or suspension.

3. *Gang-related issues:* Students who show any gang affiliation (e.g., tattoos, gang slogans, gang-related statements or gestures) will be suspended immediately pending a parent conference and/or hearing with a district police officer.

4. *Racial and sexual harassment:* Verbal, physical, or written statements involving sexual harassment or racial harassment will result in immediate suspension.

5. *Hugging and other physical contact:* Hugging and other physical contact are inappropriate at school and will result in lunch detention.

6. *Unexcused absences:* Unexcused absences will be made up in after-school detentions. Cumulative unexcused absences will result in enforcement of state attendance laws.

7. *Tardies:* Students who are not in their seats when the bell rings will be assigned a lunch detention. Cumulative violations will result in after-school detention and parent conferences.

8. *Hall passes:* Students in the hallway during class time must have a teacher-issued hall pass.

9. *Gum chewing:* Gum chewing is not allowed and will result in lunch detention.

10. *Food and beverages:* Food and beverages are not allowed in the hallways.

11. *Beepers, pagers, cellular phones, laser pointers, personal radios, CD players, electronic devices, cameras:* These items are not allowed at school and will be confiscated. Parents may pick up confiscated beepers, cellular phones, and laser pointers. Students may pick up other items after two weeks.

12. *Skateboards and roller blades:* Skateboards and roller blades are not allowed at school. If students bring these items to school, they will be confiscated. Students may pick them up after two weeks.

13. *Skipping class or being removed from after-school detention:* Students who skip class or must be removed from after-school detention due to disciplinary problems will be placed in Friday school.

14. *Athletes who receive after-school detention or Friday school:* Athletes who are placed in after-school detention or Friday school will miss one athletic event.

15. *Lateness:* Students who are late to school due to a nonemergency, such as missing the bus or getting up late, will receive lunch detention that day.

16. *Dance attendance:* Students who are suspended or placed in Friday school will not be allowed to attend one dance.

FIGURE 10.2

BUILDINGWIDE SIGNAL

"Give me your attention, please" means the following:

- Feet flat on the floor
- Eyes looking forward at the speaker
- Hands still
- Ears listening
- Mouths quiet

Provide Support for Substitutes

The challenge of coming into a new classroom where the students are unfamiliar and classroom procedures are new can be huge for substitute teachers. Students should be taught that they must treat a substitute as respectfully as they treat their regular teacher. Among the many ways classroom teachers can help substitutes are the following:

- Maintaining an accurate seating chart
- Identifying a staff member substitutes can check with if they need help
- Listing the classroom/buildingwide consequences for rule violations
- Communicating to students the expectation that they are to behave for substitutes the same way they should behave for their teacher
- Asking a neighboring teacher to take the most difficult students while the substitute is in the classroom

11

Monitoring Strategies

Once you have established clear parameters for acceptable student behaviors, you need to ensure that students are following them. In Chapter 3, we discussed four main monitoring strategies that should be part of every teacher's repertoire. In this chapter, we cover some additional monitoring strategies for reducing the number of discipline problems in your school.

Move Around the Room

Moving around the room to maintain proximity with individual students was thoroughly reviewed during the discussion of monitoring skills in Section 1. Its power and impact are so significant that we are listing it again as a "can't-miss" approach and including some more specific examples of how to put it into practice.

Ask yourself how you can arrange desks to make it easier to get close to your students, thereby eliminating barriers between you and them. Marzano (2003) identifies these critical criteria for room arrangement:

- You can easily see all students.
- Students can easily see all presentations and demonstrations.
- Frequently used materials are easily accessible.
- Pathways facilitate traffic flow.
- It is easy to organize students into pairs, triads, and small groups.
- The room does not provide or highlight unnecessary distractions. (p. 94)

Student desks or tables should be arranged so that it is easy for you to quickly move into close proximity to any student at any time during instruction. The next few figures show several examples of arrangements that let you do just that. In Figure 11.1, the teacher can easily move up to every desk in the classroom, can walk between all the desks to get closer to the students, and can even teach from the front, center, or back of the classroom. This arrangement can be used at elementary and secondary levels.

FIGURE 11.1

DESK ARRANGEMENT

Figure 11.2 shows a common arrangement used in classrooms in which students are seated at tables. In this arrangement, the teacher can easily monitor two aisles of tables by walking between the rows. This can be used at either the elementary or secondary levels.

FIGURE 11.2

TABLE ARRANGEMENT

Figure 11.3 shows a U-shaped table arrangement that provides for easy accessibility to students and close monitoring by the teacher. This arrangement is especially useful and effective in a classroom in which there are many student discussions.

FIGURE 11.3

U-SHAPED TABLE ARRANGEMENT

A major question that needs to be addressed in setting up the classroom is, *Where should the teacher's desk go?* Thompson (1998) says that an obvious mistake that many teachers make is placing their desks at the front of the room. She says it's better practice to place the desk at the back of the room or in one of the back corners because then teachers can monitor students without letting them know they're being watched. You need to consider which is the best for your classroom.

In summary, the position and arrangement of student desks or tables and the teacher's desk can have an impact on the teacher's ability to monitor students and is worth careful thought and consideration.

Call on Students at Any Time

During teacher-led discussions, it is important for every student to be actively thinking about the topic that is being discussed. If students know they will not be required to participate in the discussion, they are more likely to be off task. You have to be certain that your instructional style does not communicate that you will not call on certain students during class discussions. Usually there are students who look bored, rarely volunteer a response, or typically struggle with response opportunities. When you fail to call on these students, there is an increased likelihood that they will remain disinterested in the topic and be off task.

One of the most common ways teachers "give permission" for students to tune out is by communicating that if they keep their hands down, they will not be required to participate in the discussions. There is nothing wrong with calling on students with their hands raised, but it can create problems if you call exclusively on students with their hands raised. Employing a balanced approach by calling on students whether their hands are raised or down helps to keep all the students attentive and on task.

Following is a list of some of the common mistakes to avoid when calling on students:

- Using a set and predictable pattern (e.g., starting with names that begin with "A")
- Calling a student's name before asking the question
- Calling on the same student repeatedly and not calling on other students
- Calling on a student only once over a long period of time
- Only calling on students with their hands raised

Some strategies that you can use to communicate to your students that any of them could be called on at any time include the following:

- Draw student names at random.
- Call on students with their hands down more often than those with their hands raised.
- Direct all students to give the answer to the question to their neighbors.
- Require every student to write the answers to your questions on scratch paper or on individual blackboards.

Eliminate Blind Spots During Classroom Transitions

Far too often, teachers allow students to become spread out as they transition from one location in the building to the next. Also, teachers often escort students through the building in a manner that limits their direct view of the students. This typically happens as students go around corners or enter rooms. In these scenarios, blind spots are inevitable, and problems can occur while the teacher is not monitoring the situation.

It is important that your students do not get too spread out when moving from one building location to the next. Escorting your students in a manner that maximizes your ability to directly observe them as they go around building corners is also beneficial. Telling the first student in line to stop at a corner or door entrance until you get to that spot does a great deal to eliminate blind spots. Finally, walking behind the students during transition periods helps you keep every student in your direct line of sight.

Go to the Students When They Need Help

In some classrooms, students are instructed to go to the teacher's desk when they need help with their seat work. This procedure is unwise and can create many classroom problems. Students often visit with friends and cause disruptions as they walk to the teacher's desk. Because the students wait for your assistance at a location other than their desks, time that could have been productive if they had remained at their desks and continued working while waiting is wasted. Students who are lined up at your desk also can block your view of the rest of the class—this makes it difficult to monitor the class.

You should consider implementing a policy that requires students to raise their hands when they need help. A system that some teachers use is that students put up a small "help flag" when they need help. The teacher can then move from desk to desk to provide the needed assistance. A strategy that Wong and Wong (1998) suggest is giving each student a toilet paper tube that has been painted red on one end so that they can stand the tube with the red side up when they need help. Another strategy they suggest is using an index card that says "Help" on one side and "Keep working" on the other. Students are taught that when they need help, they put the card up with the "Help" side facing the teacher and the "Keep working" side facing the student—a call for help from the teacher and a reminder to the student to keep working until the teacher comes over.

Maximize Wait Time

The goal during class discussions is to get students thinking about the topic being discussed and preparing to answer any question they might be asked. The time that elapses between the moment you ask the entire class a question and the moment you call on an individual student is prime thinking time because all the students realize they might be called on to answer the question.

Sometimes when conducting class discussions, teachers will pose a question to the entire class but then immediately call on an individual student. This lets all the other students off the hook, allowing them not to have to think about the question. Prolong the wait time before calling on someone. When you increase the time period during which students feel they might be responsible for answering a specific question, you are also increasing the amount of time students will intently think about the question. Also, when you use this strategy consistently, it shows that you have high expectations for everyone (Kerman et al., 1980).

Correct Nondisruptive Off-Task Behavior

It is important to note and correct off-task behavior, even when a student engaging in such behavior is not bothering anyone else. Examples include situations in which students passively resist the teacher's instructions, daydream during class discussions, sleep, write notes, or doodle.

It's easy to ignore nondisruptive off-task behaviors because they typically don't cause a classroom disturbance or distract other students. However, ignoring them has a number of negative effects. First, the student who is involved in the nondisruptive behavior remains off task and is not involved in the learning process. Also, as other students observe that such behavior is ignored by the teacher, they absorb the message that these actions are acceptable.

One of the easiest and most effective monitoring techniques you can use to quickly stop nondisruptive off-task behavior is proximity. Moving toward a student who is on the wrong page or daydreaming will usually bring him or her back to the class discussion. If monitoring procedures fail to stop the nondisruptive off-task behavior, you should employ other strategies to nip the problem in the bud.

Take Roll Silently

Many teachers start class by calling the name of each student as they take roll. This process takes a significant amount of time away from classroom instruction, decreases the ability to monitor students, and creates a potential for disruption. When hearing their names called off, students can respond in a way that is inappropriate. Statements such as "Yeah," "What do you want?" and "He's over there" are some examples.

A better approach is to have the students begin an assignment the moment they enter the room. While the students are completing their assignment, you can check your seating chart and silently take roll.

Another alternative some teachers use is for students to "take their own roll" by moving their names on a chart, placing it either on the side indicating they are buying lunch or on the side indicating they are not buying lunch. (See Figure 11.4 for illustrations of such a system.) This can be done silently as students enter the room. The names left on the borders are the students who are absent. The drawback is that one student could move another student's name as a way to help out a friend.

Use Sponge Activities

Free time in class often translates to an increase in nonproductive activities and a greater likelihood of disruptive and off-task student behavior.

FIGURE 11.4

ROLL-TAKING ALTERNATIVE

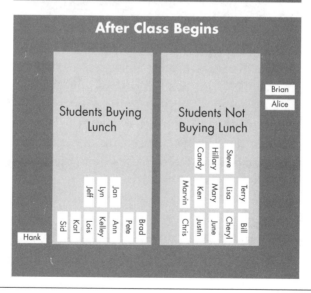

Sponge activities are learning opportunities provided for students when they might otherwise have free, unstructured class time. An example of a sponge activity is a warm-up assignment on the board that students know they are to work on as soon as they enter the classroom.

Sponge activities are typically given to students when they enter the room, during roll taking, and when students complete their work early. This is a proactive strategy that, when used routinely, decreases opportunities for students to misbehave, allows the teacher to monitor the class, and provides additional learning time for students.

Remember the Three "Make or Break" Times

There are typically three times during the day when the likelihood of students getting off task or becoming disruptive is very high: when students enter the classroom, transition times, and the last two minutes of class. These are the times when most classroom disruptions occur and when the majority of office referrals are made. It is especially important to monitor students during these times. "Make or break" times create a classroom atmosphere that can have either a negative or a positive impact on learning and classroom structure.

You should do everything possible to create and maintain a structured and orderly environment during these "make or break" times. Some ways to do this include avoiding free time altogether, teaching routines and procedures for transitions, continually monitoring your students, and maintaining an academic focus during these times.

Change Hall Passes

It is inevitable that some students will steal hall passes and use them without permission. Changing the color of hall passes each month on a buildingwide basis will make old hall passes useless.

Encourage Students to Leave the Building

Often students will walk through the halls and attempt to enter classrooms long after the school day is finished. These students create supervision problems and distractions for staff. A good way to encourage the students to leave at the end of the day is for the principal to go on the public address system 15 minutes after the final bell and remind students they are to leave the building if they are not involved in an organized school activity. Informing students that if they remain in the hallways they will receive lunch detention can give them a strong incentive to leave.

Stagger Passing Periods

When large numbers of students are in the hallways at any one time, the likelihood of fights and disruptions increases dramatically. Also, it can be very difficult for staff to supervise that many students. Staggering the passing periods in order to lessen the number of students transitioning at one time can help to improve student behavior and improve supervision issues.

12

Consequence Strategies

Even when staff members use all of the prevention strategies, there will still be a need for consequences. In Chapter 4, we talked about some consequences that teachers can use independent of the buildingwide discipline plan. In Chapter 7, we developed buildingwide consequences that we believe should be in place to support and back up classroom discipline plans. In this chapter, we address specific strategies that we believe teachers should use when they deliver consequences to students. These strategies increase the effectiveness of the consequences and decrease the chance that small problems will become larger problems or that power struggles will occur between staff members and students.

Tolerate No Exceptions

A teacher who gives instructions but then fails to require 100 percent compliance with those instructions is one who has a weak discipline system. After giving a directive, such as "Turn to page 14" or "Everyone, look this way," you should always check for total student compliance. If a directive is important enough to give, it's important enough to follow through on. When you let just one student fail to follow instructions, you are inadvertently telling all your students that your words are not important.

> **Tip Box**
>
> One of the best ways to increase the likelihood of student compliance is to show courtesy and respect.

Also, when one student fails to comply with a directive, it is almost inevitable that others will also fail to comply.

Pay Attention Even to Little Problems

Most teachers do a good job of enforcing the "big" rules such as "no fighting" and "follow staff instructions." The same is not always true for less significant rule infractions, such as littering or minor shoving in the hallway. Any time you fail to enforce a rule, no matter how small it might be, you are undermining the entire discipline system. McEwan and Damer (2000) state, "Tackling the small stuff while it is still manageable will foster a school environment in which the catastrophic problems are far less likely to occur" (p. 8).

There is a strong chance that when you fail to enforce "small" rule violations, more serious problems will occur in the future. Minor shoving in the hallway becomes hitting, one student talking out of turn becomes four students talking out of turn, and a little littering becomes serious graffiti.

Ideally, the entire staff should be committed to enforcing all building rules. While the severity of the consequence should be proportional to the rule violation (i.e., sometimes a verbal reminder is a sufficient response), the decision to intervene should not be related to the rule's seriousness. The bottom line is that if it's a rule, it needs to be enforced.

Keep Your Physical Distance When Disciplining

Sometimes when teachers discipline students, the teachers can become very frustrated and emotional. These situations can cause them to overreact by grabbing a student or being physical in other ways. This should be avoided if at all possible.

The only time you are justified in physically intervening with students is when they pose a clear threat to another student, a staff member, or themselves. Even during these times, you should use the minimal amount of physical force needed to make certain everyone is safe. You should also consider your own safety before intervening.

Resorting to physical contact with students often creates an entirely new problem that goes beyond the original issue. In some cases, a teacher will be subsequently put on the defensive by angry parents who insist that the teacher had no right to touch their child. Also, parents can claim that the physical intervention caused injuries to the child. In these cases, the teacher involved must prove that the physical intervention was justified and was not an overreaction. If a teacher does need to use force, he or she must immediately document exactly what happened and report it to an administrator in case it becomes a bigger issue.

Refrain from Punishing the Whole Group

Teachers typically have the best of intentions when they discipline an entire class for the actions of one student. Requiring the entire class to put their heads down, giving them detention, or giving them extra work are examples of some of the ways this is done. This practice is usually a desperate attempt to entice the class to turn in the violator.

Despite these good intentions, however, group punishments are unfair to the innocent students. Also, group punishments often create parent and student animosity toward the teacher. If you believe group punishments are justified, ask yourself the question, "Would I like to be punished for something another staff member did?" The answer is undoubtedly "no." This alone is reason enough not to take part in this type of discipline.

Don't Let Students Become "Attorneys"

If given the opportunity, many students will argue a consequence to death. This wastes your time, interrupts instruction, and becomes a show for the other students. There is no law that says a student has the right to argue about a consequence. If a rule and its consequence have been clearly communicated, due process has been used, and the student has obviously broken the rule, the time for arguing is over.

Curwin and Mendler (1988) suggest that if students feel strongly that they have been unjustifiably punished, they can be given the opportunity to fill out an appeal form that you can review later. The Consequence Appeal form, an example of which appears in Figure 12.1, provides students with an opportunity to appeal without taking your time. The form can be kept in a corner of the room, and students should be informed that if they truly feel the need to appeal a consequence, they should fill out all the information on the form and then wait for your final decision.

FIGURE 12.1

CONSEQUENCE APPEAL FORM

Name: _____

Date: _____

What rule did I violate?

_____

_____

What consequence did I receive?

_____

_____

Why should my consequence be changed, and what should it be changed to?

_____

_____

Take Notice of Misbehavior

Some teachers believe that the best way to stop misbehavior is to ignore it. This philosophical approach is based on the mistaken belief that most students disrupt the class in an effort to get the teacher's attention. But students misbehave to get attention from their peers, not their teacher. Thus, misbehavior is self-rewarding and ignoring it has no impact. It is important to follow up on all misbehaviors in a fair and consistent manner.

Assign Lunch Detention for Tardies

Students who are late to class by even a second should receive lunch detention. This process is quick, easy, and powerful. It communicates that learning time is important and will not be wasted. When this consequence is applied consistently throughout the building, the number of tardies throughout the school will decrease significantly.

End of Section Reflection Questions

1. What steps can you take to communicate positive expectations to all your students, even those who are struggling?

2. What are some rules of conduct or discipline plan policies that need to be taught or retaught to your students at this time of year?
3. Which of the classroom monitoring strategies could you do a better job of implementing: proximity, silence, use of the eyes, or response opportunities?
4. After reviewing all the consequence strategies, which would you like to focus on and why?

THE
CHALLENGING
STUDENT

The Challenging Student

Every school and every classroom has students whose behavior is extremely difficult to control. According to Adelman and Taylor (2002), between 12 and 22 percent of all children in schools suffer from mental, emotional, or behavioral disorders. Many of these students are the ones who don't respond to the routine strategies and behavior expectations that work with the rest of the class. These students create severe challenges to teachers and other staff members on a regular basis. Acts of defiance, noncompliance, belligerence, inattentiveness, constant movement, and continual talking out of turn are just some of the behaviors exhibited by these students.

Whereas some challenging students have had thorough assessments and have been given a special education label, many have not. From the teacher's standpoint, this makes it more difficult to know what to do to deal with the misbehaviors. At least when a student has been labeled and is receiving special services, a number of specific strategies have been identified and a plan has been developed to help school staff work together for the benefit of the student. When the student has not been served in this way, it is up to the teacher to determine strategies that work for that student and assist in creating a positive climate in the classroom.

We believe that some students, approximately 5 percent, come to us with specific emotional and behavioral issues that stem from their home lives or from their own particular emotional, mental, or physical disorders. The negative behaviors of another group, which makes up about 15 percent of our students, is a result of poor classroom management. This is consistent with Curwin and Mendler's (1988) 80-15-5 principle, in which they state that 80 percent of students rarely break the rules, 15 percent of students occasionally break the rules, and 5 percent of students often break the rules. The 5 percent is the group that is especially challenging. The 5 percent can quickly increase to 20 percent, however, if you don't deal effectively with the 15 percent who are the "fence-rider" kids, those students whose behavior will get better or worse depending on your ability to effectively implement the discipline components reviewed in Sections 1, 2, and 3.

Figure S4 illustrates this principle. In the top box of the figure, A is the 80 percent of students who rarely break the rules, B is the 15 percent who occasionally break the rules, and C is the 5 percent who often break the rules. In the middle box, the percentage of students who rarely break the rules (A and B) increases to 95 percent due to the teacher's strong classroom management skills. In the bottom box, conversely, the percentage of students who often break the rules (B and C) increases to 20 percent due to the poor classroom management skills of the teacher.

FIGURE S4

EFFECTS OF STRONG VERSUS POOR CLASS MANAGEMENT

The 80-15-5 Rule

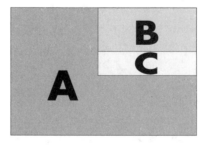

The Effects of Strong Classroom Management

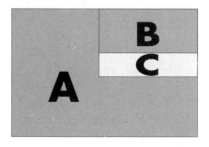

(Figure continued on next page)

FIGURE S4

EFFECTS OF STRONG VERSUS POOR CLASS MANAGEMENT
(CONTINUED)

The Effects of Poor Classroom Management

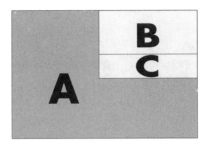

In this section, our goal is to help you make your classroom look like the one represented by the middle box in Figure S4. We will begin by covering relationship and climate strategies, academic strategies, and disciplinary strategies to use with your challenging students. Then we will discuss how to respond to classroom disruptions and to major rule violations. Next, we identify specific strategies for working with students who have anger management issues, oppositional defiant disorder (ODD), or attention deficit hyperactivity disorder (ADHD).

There are a couple of points to keep in mind as you read the chapters on dealing with specific disorders. First of all, look at the behavior of your students when determining what strategies to use, not the labels assigned to students. For example, some students will exhibit the behaviors of a student with ODD without having the label. Second, one size does not fit all, so try different strategies mentioned to see what works for your students. Even the experts do not agree on what strategies always work with different behavior disorders. Finally, the strategies reviewed in this section, although specific to the identified disorder, can also help you work successfully with all students. Marzano (2003) says, "Effective managers do not treat all students the same, particularly in situations involving behavior problems. Whereas some students need encouragement, other students need a gentle reprimand, and still others might require a not-so-gentle reprimand" (p. 48). It is important to know what will work with which students and to keep the underlying goal of positive teacher-student relations in mind with all students.

The final and possibly most important point to remember is that you should always treat the challenging student, as well as all students, with dignity. Curwin and Mendler (1988) state that survivors of concentration camps said the most important thing for them was to hold their heads high and maintain their dignity. They further state that in schools, students should know that no matter what, their dignity will be preserved.

13

Dealing with Challenging Students

We will begin this chapter by quickly reviewing strategies that can be used for challenging students, regardless of their diagnosis. Remember not only that you should determine which strategies work for your particular students but also that many of these strategies work well with all students. We have categorized these into relationship/climate strategies, academic strategies, and disciplinary strategies.

Relationship/Climate Strategies

Gradually Assign Responsibility and Leadership

Tauber (1999) states that when you give challenging students responsibility and a leadership role, you can help them turn their negative self-concept into one that is positive and their obstructive actions into helpful ones. Of course, there is a danger that this technique could backfire, so do this gradually, moving from small, private responsibilities toward larger and more visible ones. You could start off by having a student take messages to the office for you. If this succeeds, you could give the student more visible responsibilities, such as assigning him or her to tutor a less capable student.

Display a Personal Interest Daily

The challenging student is more difficult to bond with and often has few adult relationships. As a teacher, it is important that you go out of your way to show your students that you like and value them. Simply going out of your way to greet your challenging students each morning or asking them questions about sports or hobbies they are interested in is a way to display that interest, which in turn fosters positive relationships.

Drop All Grudges

Don't take a student's negative actions personally (Tauber, 1999). Anything he does or says does not have to do with you. It has to do with him and the particular disorder he has. Holding grudges only exacerbates the situation.

Limit Negative Faculty Room Talk

When teachers go to the faculty room and spend their time complaining about difficult students, they are contributing to the negative cycle of interactions between staff members and students. This is counterproductive to what needs to happen to improve relations with these students. Using this time to problem solve or hear from other staff members about techniques that work may be beneficial, but complaining and spreading bad feelings is not a good idea.

Open Parent Conferences with a Positive Statement

This strategy, mentioned earlier as a technique to use during all parent conferences, is especially critical with conferences with parents of the most challenging students. These parents are so programmed to hearing negative things about their child that they often come to meetings ready to fight. You can totally disarm them at the beginning of the conference by sincerely sharing something that you like about the student or something positive about their child they may not be aware of.

Tell the Student You Understand Her Feelings

Validating a student's feelings doesn't mean that you agree with her actions, but it helps her to know that her feelings are real, honest, and normal. Sometimes all a student wants is to know that you understand how she feels.

Value the Student, Despite the Inappropriate Action

Even when a student does something that is inappropriate and results in a consequence, remember to tell him that you like him, value him, and know that he'll make a better choice next time (Tauber, 1999).

Academic Strategies

Keep the Class Moving

Slowly paced instruction and unplanned time periods are problems waiting to happen for all students, but they are especially deadly for challenging students. Effective, appropriately fast-paced instruction will prevent many problems from occurring.

Unleash the Power of Appropriately High Expectations

Having high expectations of all students, even the students you struggle to have high expectations for, is very powerful. Research has demonstrated the power that high expectations have for all students (Kerman et al., 1980).

Disciplinary Strategies

Bargaining Is Not an Option

The challenging student is very adept at bargaining and manipulation. Success in bargaining only increases the chance that she'll repeat the offense and then try to bargain away the consequence. It is important to be firm in your implementation of consequences so that she learns she can't manipulate the situation and get away with her actions.

Criticize the Action, Not the Student

Focusing on the action and not on the student is important. There is an important distinction to be made between letting a student know that fighting is inappropriate and not allowed and telling him that he is a bad person for fighting.

Have an Emergency Response Team in Place

Challenging students have a high probability of exploding, so it is essential to have a plan in place regarding what to do to get help from an emergency response team when it is needed.

Have a Buddy Teacher Available to Help Out

There will be times when you have had your fill of a challenging student and need a break. When that happens, it works wonders to have an arrangement with a buddy teacher to whom you can send the student for a brief time out (Tauber, 1999). This will give you time to get past your frustration point and be able to once again deal with the student professionally.

Apply Immediate and Meaningful Consequences

Even more so than with most students, you need to have immediate and meaningful consequences to implement with difficult students when they get to the point that the typical relationship, parameter, and monitoring strategies are not enough. These consequences have been covered in Chapters 4 and 7.

Judge Students' Actions Fairly

It is easy to jump to conclusions with challenging students and assume they are guilty of any infraction they are accused of. Remember to be fair and look at each situation based on the current facts and information you have rather than punishing the "usual suspect."

Make the "Death Penalty" the Last Option

Sometimes you can get so frustrated and fed up with a difficult student that you want to hand down a severe consequence for even a minor offense. Remember to save the most stringent consequences for the most serious offenses.

Never Intervene Physically with a Student

It may be tempting to put your hands on a difficult student or to try to restrain her during an outburst, but this can have serious consequences for you and for the student. The only time you should intervene physically is if the student may hurt herself or someone else, and even then you should have gone through training on how to do so safely.

Provide the Student with Choices

When correcting a student's behavior, it is always more effective to give options rather than make demands. For example, instead of ordering, "Get to work!" try saying, "Do you want to work on your math or your spelling now?"

Quiet Corrections Are the Most Powerful

You should be private in your corrections of your students rather than publicly reprimand them. According to Tauber (1999), public reprimands increase the chance of escalating problems and take away the students' dignity.

Reward Students for Accomplishments, Not Promises

Challenging students are experts at diverting a responsibility or a consequence by making promises. It is vital to wait until they have actually completed a task or followed through on an assignment before rewarding them for their behavior (Tauber, 1999).

Saving Face Is Everything

Allow students to save face whenever possible, as this allows them to keep their dignity and also helps prevent issues from becoming worse. Using other strategies already mentioned, such as giving choices and correcting privately, are ways that you can allow students to save face (Tauber, 1999).

Responding to Classroom Disruptions

Every teacher has to deal with classroom disruptions on a daily basis. When these are dealt with effectively, consistently, and immediately, the chances of their escalating and spreading is greatly reduced. Examples of typical classroom disruptions are talking out of turn, interrupting, bothering others, out-of-seat behaviors, turning around in class, and failure to comply with the teacher's signal.

This chapter will cover how to progressively respond to these disruptions, moving up a hierarchy of responses as the situation calls for it. This hierarchy begins with responding nonverbally and moves to responding verbally, then making demands, and, finally, implementing consequences. This response hierarchy is illustrated in Figure 14.1.

FIGURE 14.1

RESPONSE HIERARCHY

Nonverbal Interventions
Planned ignoring and monitoring (proximity, silence, a "look")

↓

Verbal Interventions
Inferential statements, student's name, asking questions, "I" statements

↓

Demands

↓

Consequences

There are guidelines you should keep in mind as you respond to classroom disruptions:

- Always protect the safety of all students, including the disruptive student.
- Use the technique requiring the least intervention that will still be sufficient to address the problem rather than go overboard in your response.
- Be sure that your response doesn't cause more of a disturbance than the student's disruption does.
- Encourage students to examine their behavior and make an appropriate choice.

Shrigley (1985) says that 40 percent of classroom disruptions can be handled appropriately through the use of nonverbal responses by the teacher. Two types of nonverbal responses are planned ignoring and use of monitoring techniques. There are a couple of examples in which planned ignoring can be effective. For instance, if you tell your students, "When you clear your desks, I'll hand out your papers," and one student doesn't clear his desk, give papers to every student but him until he complies. You can also tell your class, "In this discussion, I want you to raise your hand when I ask a question." If one student blurts out the answer, ignore her and call on another student who is raising her hand.

Planned ignoring may work in a few situations, but a more effective nonverbal response that can be applied in most situations is monitoring. This includes a combination of proximity, silence, and a "look." If a student is ignoring your signal when you say, "Give me your attention, please," walk up to the student, say nothing, and look at him as you wait for him to comply. Most of the time, these actions are enough to get the response you're looking for.

When nonverbal interventions don't work, you need to move up the hierarchy to verbal intervention. There are seven guidelines for verbal interventions: make sure they are private, maintain proximity, remain calm in your approach, communicate respect and courtesy to the student, speak about the situation and not the student, give specific directions rather than speak in generalities, and intervene in a timely manner.

The first four guidelines are fairly clear. However, there may be confusion about the last three, so we will look at some examples:

- *Speak about the situation and not the student:* "John, it is disrespect-ful to be talking when I have asked for your attention. Give me your attention now."
- *Give specific directions:* "Celia, when I ask for your attention, I want you to put your pencil down and look at me."
- *Intervene in a timely manner:* "David, I just asked you to give me your attention. Please do so now."

There are four types of verbal interventions you can use: making infer-ential statements, calmly saying the student's name, asking questions, and using "I" statements. When using inferential statements, you make your expectations known in an indirect rather than a direct way. The benefit of this is that it can prevent confrontation and embarrassment. For example, you might say, "As soon as everyone puts their books away, we can start working on our science project." This keeps you from having to single out a specific student for attention. Another approach is to calmly say a student's name to redirect his attention. If you have given your signal and the entire class has complied except for Carrie, you calmly say, "Carrie." This often is enough to have the student comply. You can also ask a ques-tion: "Michael, are you aware that I'm waiting to get your attention?" And finally, you can use "I" statements. "Sara, I asked for everyone's attention and I'm still waiting for you to comply. This bothers me because I want everyone to be ready for the science project."

Going up the response hierarchy, we move from verbal interventions to demands. Demands should be used when nonverbal and verbal interven-tions have not been effective. It is essential that when you make demands, you use a firm and calm voice, maintain eye contact, and speak to the stu-dent in a private, rather than public, way. Say specifically and directly what the student is to do: "Jane, turn around and give me your attention now." At this point, it is vital that you don't explain or justify your demand. Nor should you bargain, argue, or plead with the student.

When nonverbal interventions, verbal interventions, and demands don't work, it is time to move up the hierarchy to consequences. When applying consequences, you must be assertive but not aggressive. Aggres-sive actions include making "you" statements, such as, "You are getting a detention"; putting your body in too close proximity to the student; pub-licly doling out a consequence in front of the class; humiliating a student;

and displaying negative facial expressions. On the other hand, assertive communication can be helped by using a firm voice, maintaining eye contact, using the student's name, speaking slowly and calmly, and being as private as possible while giving the consequence.

Before you reach the consequence level in the hierarchy, you must have already determined what the appropriate consequence should be. As stated earlier, you should be sure that the consequence fits the student's action and not go overboard in what you deliver. Examples of consequences may include processing, student conference, parent conference, office referral, or detention, as reviewed in Chapters 4 and 7.

Let's look at an example of a situation in which you would give a consequence for student misbehavior. Imagine that you have asked for the attention of the class, and all students have complied except for Terry. You have tried nonverbal interventions, verbal interventions, and demands, with no response from Terry. At this point, you walk up to Terry and very quietly and privately say, "Terry, I have asked you repeatedly to give me your attention and you have failed to do so. Go to Room 104 for processing now, please." The happy ending to the story is that at this point Terry knows you mean business and quickly complies. However, if he responds with, "That's not fair. You don't make anyone else do that," you should very calmly repeat your directive: "Terry, that's not the point. Go to Room 104 now." If he says, "That's not fair. I'm not going," the problem has escalated and he is now noncompliant. At this point, you increase the consequence because of the new issue of noncompliance. You then say something like, "Terry, I've told you twice to go to Room 104 and you have not complied. Pick up your things and go to the office now."

In summary, it is important to intervene with classroom disruptions so that a minimal amount of interference with instruction takes place. When necessary, however, you should move up the response hierarchy from nonverbal interventions, to verbal interventions, to demands, and finally to consequences.

In the next chapter, we will cover things you need to know when dealing with major rule violations. This includes how to deal with power struggles, how to determine what the truth is, how to interview witnesses, and standards for determining guilt.

15

Dealing with Major Rule Violations

Teachers can experience "burnout" when major rule violations occur on a frequent basis, especially when the teachers don't have strategies in place to deal with them. Major rule violations include power struggles between students and teachers, fights, theft, drug or alcohol use, and weapons violations. In this chapter, we will introduce an alternative to power struggles that can help you de-escalate the situation and work toward a positive conclusion. We will also share ideas about how to promote student honesty and cover how to work with students when you need witnesses to determine what has happened. When you have these plans to rely on, you are suddenly in control and even the most difficult rule violation is solvable.

Power Struggles

In dealing with challenging students, it is inevitable that a student will attempt to draw you into a power struggle. For the purposes of our discussion, we define a power struggle as a conflict between two or more persons in which the participants are attempting to control the actions and attitudes of the other with behaviors such as intimidation, threats, or defiance. Often, the power struggle results in grandstanding by the student, further escalation of a negative situation, and a no-win situation for both you and the student. As a professional educator, it is very important that you are aware of when a student is attempting to draw you into a power struggle and that you don't take the bait.

Students who engage in power struggles often have a disrespect for authority, are not affected by threats, and like to play to their audience.

How do teachers respond to this combination? Often, they panic and over-react if they don't have a plan in place or experience in dealing with power struggles. Tauber (1999) says that the typical teacher initially responds to such a situation with an increase in blood pressure, feelings of frustration and anger, irrational threats, and a raised voice. The teacher may choose one of two responses to the student: fight back or give in.

Let's look at a typical power struggle scenario. Mr. Edwards has told his student, Frank, to get to work. Frank defiantly responds that he won't and Mr. Edwards can't make him. If Mr. Edwards chooses to fight back, the dialogue between the two may go something like this:

> *Mr. Edwards:* "Frank, please get to work and stop wasting time."
>
> *Frank:* "This work is stupid, and I'm not going to do it!"
>
> *Mr. Edwards:* "Frank, I said to get to work now!"
>
> *Frank:* "Why should I? This is stupid and I won't do it!"
>
> *Mr. Edwards:* "That's not the point. Get to work *now,* mister!"
>
> *Frank:* "I'll get to work when I'm ready!"
>
> *Mr. Edwards:* "Wrong. You'll get to work now!"
>
> *Frank:* "You're the one who's wrong! Are you deaf? I said I'd get to work when I'm ready!"
>
> *Mr. Edwards:* "That's it! You're out of here! Get going!"
>
> *Frank:* "Boy, that's just what I wanted. I hate this dumb class." He storms out of the room, slamming the door.

There is no winner in this scenario. The teacher modeled inappropriate behaviors for the rest of the class, instruction was disrupted, the classroom atmosphere was damaged, the relationship between the teacher and student was hurt, and the student will very likely be suspended from school.

A scenario in which the teacher gives in goes something like this:

> *Mr. Edwards:* "Frank, please get to work."
>
> *Frank:* "This work is stupid, and I'm not going to do it!"
>
> *Mr. Edwards:* "Frank, this work is important, and I really want you to do it."
>
> *Frank:* "Why should I? I'm bored and I'm not doing it."

Mr. Edwards: "I'm sorry you feel that way. I really wish you would do it."

Frank: "I'll get to work when I'm ready, and I'm not ready now!"

Mr. Edwards: "That's fine. I hope you're ready soon."

There is no winner in this scenario, either. The teacher is disempowered, frustrated, and embarrassed. The student has gained power by doing whatever he wants, and he will probably repeat his actions in the future. He has modeled inappropriate behavior for the other students and possibly gained their respect. The teacher's overall authority has been questioned and devalued, and there's a strong likelihood that other students will try this type of behavior in the future.

There is a third option that is a more appropriate response for dealing with power struggles. We term this the power struggle alternative, adapted from Tauber (1999) and Walker and Walker (1991). To put this process into practice, you must follow these steps:

1. Disengage your emotions.
2. De-escalate the situation.
3. Admit the student's power.
4. Review alternatives.

To disengage your emotions, take a deep breath, depersonalize the situation by reminding yourself that it isn't about you, and give yourself a personal time out. To de-escalate the situation, use supportive nonverbal gestures such as keeping your hands down by your side, putting space between you and the student, and talking in a private location if at all possible. Your verbal responses should also be supportive: speak in a calm, quiet voice, use the student's name, and offer assistance to the student. Tauber (1999) points out that the student's motivation is getting power over the situation and you and suggests that you should let him have it by admitting that you can't make him do anything.

Here is a possible scenario in which Mr. Edwards successfully implements the power struggle alternative with Frank:

Mr. Edwards: "Frank, please get to work."

Frank: "This work is stupid, and I'm not going to do it."

Mr. Edwards: "Frank, is there a part of the work that is difficult? I'll give you a hand and help you with it."

Frank: "You can't help me!"

Mr. Edwards: "I'm sorry you feel that way. You need to do the work anyway."

Frank: "Forget it! You can't make me do it!"

Mr. Edwards: "You're right. I can't make you do it. I certainly hope you decide to do it because if you waste your time and don't do it here, you will be choosing to do it after school in detention. Let me know what you decide. I'll check back with you in a few minutes."

At this point, the teacher walks away to give the student space and returns in a few minutes to see what he has decided to do. This gives both Mr. Edwards and Frank a time out and increases the chance that Frank will make the positive choice of getting to work. If, however, he doesn't, the teacher needs to be prepared to follow through with the promised consequence of after-school detention.

Student Honesty

It is very important for the entire staff to encourage student honesty. This is not only a quality that contributes to good citizenship; it also protects innocent students, saves our time, and saves the time of witnesses. The truth is that many students struggle with telling the truth, and this is especially a problem with challenging students.

There are several reasons why students may be dishonest when involved in a serious rule violation. First of all, they may have found it to work for them in the past. Second, they realize that if they persist in being dishonest, teachers will give up. Third, they may be concerned about how their parents will respond when they find out what they did. Fourth, they want to avoid the consequence for their misbehavior. And finally, they may even have convinced themselves that they are innocent.

Four approaches can help promote honesty when working with students. Fostering trusting and positive relationships with all of your students, creating a reputation for finding out the truth behind rule violations, holding honesty discussions in your classroom, and making specific statements that promote student honesty all go a long way toward encouraging your students to tell the truth.

We covered the importance of fostering trusting and positive relationships with all students in Chapter 1; the most powerful strategies are those that demonstrate how much you care about each and every one of your students. Welcoming them as they enter your classroom, listening intently and sincerely when they share something personal about themselves, making a point to know something about each of them, and talking to them about their special talents are all ways to foster positive relationships and build trust.

Teachers gain reputations for finding out the truth behind rule violations when they consistently work to solve those violations. Students notice when teachers do this; even when the violations don't involve them, they learn through observation that it doesn't pay to break the rules because the teacher will determine the truth and deal appropriately with the rule violator.

Discussing honesty with the entire class is something that we encourage you to do periodically as needed. In these discussions, you should emphasize that everyone makes mistakes and that that is just part of life. What is more important is how you deal with a mistake after you have made it. You should also stress that lying is neither inevitable nor the best or most appropriate course of action after making a mistake. The truth is that if a student lies, she will receive a consequence not only for the mistake that she made but also for lying. On the other hand, if she tells the truth, that will have a positive effect on the consequence for the mistake.

There are seven statement types that we have found to be successful as you work with students to get them to tell the truth. When making any of these statements, you should be calm in your approach, make direct eye contact, speak with the student in a private location, and be certain not to threaten the student.

The first type of statement is use of the "one foot analogy." This approach is one that can be effective with a visual learner. Say something like, "If you make a mistake and are honest about it, you will be in this much trouble." You hold up your hands about one foot apart in front of the student. "However, if you lie to me, you will be in this much trouble." You then move your hands apart at least another foot to visually illustrate how the student's trouble can grow.

The second type of statement is one that works well with students who like math or like to play the odds: "If you made a mistake and are honest, you will get a certain consequence. However, if you made a mistake and lie about it, I will double the consequence because of the lie."

The third type of statement is one you may use with a student who you know is basically honest or a student who hates confrontation. This is the "look me in the eye" approach: "I am going to ask you a question. When you answer, I want you to look me straight in the eye and tell me the truth. If you lie, not only will I be terribly disappointed that you lied, but also your trouble will increase."

The fourth type of statement is one to use with a student who you know is worried about how his parents will react: "When I ask you about a rule that was broken, you need to tell me the truth. I really hope you are honest. If you aren't honest, when I call your parents I will first tell them about the rule you broke. If you think they will be angry about that, wait until I have to tell them that you lied to me about it."

The fifth statement type is useful with a student who is generally responsible. In this approach, you say, "I'm really busy and have a very full schedule today. When I ask you about a rule that was broken, you need to be honest because no matter how busy I am, I am going to take all of the time I need to find the truth."

The sixth type of statement is one that is useful with a student who realizes that there are witnesses who will turn him in: "In a minute, I am going to ask you a question about a rule that was broken. When you answer, whatever you do, don't lie to me. If I need to, I will interview as many kids as necessary until I find the truth."

The final approach is usually effective for the challenging student. In this approach, you say something like, "I am going to ask you a question about a rule that was broken. Before you answer, remember that I will eventually find out the truth. I always do. I will interview witnesses and check all the facts until I discover the truth. So the best thing is to be honest with me."

Determining Guilt

Even with this arsenal of strategies to get students to be honest and confess to wrongdoing, there will always be some who won't tell the truth. This leaves you to determine who is guilty of the infraction.

There are three circumstances that effectively prove guilt in the school setting. In the first circumstance, if the situation was witnessed by a staff member, you can complete your investigation after getting a clear statement from the staff member of exactly what he or she witnessed. Don't be enticed by parents or the student into taking the word of a student over the word of a staff member. The second circumstance occurs when there is irrefutable evidence, such as a student found holding a stolen item. The third circumstance involves collecting strong statements from witnesses.

In working with witnesses, there are several things to keep in mind. First of all, witnesses should have the right to remain anonymous. Second, be sure to use only credible witnesses, that is, students you know to have a history of being honest. Third, interviews with students should be held in private. Finally, you should have at least three witnesses saying the same thing. Fewer corroborating statements than that will be damaging to your case.

There are times and situations in which students don't want to be witnesses, especially as they get older. Understanding the reasons for this is important so that you can work with all students to dispel the myths that contribute to their refusal to be witnesses. There is often the perception that if students report wrongdoing, they are a "rat" or a "narc." The reality that you should teach your students is that a "rat" only tells on someone to get them into trouble. A witness tells on someone to right a wrong or to help the offending student in the long run. A second reason that a student may struggle with being a witness is that she doesn't want to get her friend in trouble. The reality that should be taught to your students is that when they are a witness to a serious rule violation, they are helping their friend in the long run to get the help that he or she needs. A third reason a student may not want to be a witness is that he is afraid he will get beat up. In this case, you need to assure the student that you will keep his identity anonymous and that he will be protected from the other student or students. A fourth reason a student may hesitate to be a witness is that she is afraid she will be the only witness. In this case, you should reassure her that you intend to have at least three statements from witnesses before determining guilt. It is critical that after a serious rule violation in which you used witnesses to prove a student's guilt, you check back with the witnesses to be certain they are doing all right and that they are safe.

16

Students with Anger Management Issues

An important life skill for students to learn is how to control their anger in an appropriate and acceptable manner. Unfortunately, most classrooms have at least one student who has a great deal of trouble handling his or her anger. Typically, these students shout, rebel, become defiant, and break school rules when they are angry or frustrated. These students are very much at risk of school failure and problems in life if they do not learn how to deal with their emotions in acceptable ways. In addition, they can have a devastating impact on the classroom environment, interfere with learning by other students, and create extreme teacher frustration and job dissatisfaction. A teacher's reaction to a student's anger can either de-escalate the situation or intensify the student's outburst.

In this chapter, we will review strategies and consequences to use with students who have anger management issues.

Approaches for Working with Anger

It is easy for a teacher to become angry and frustrated when dealing with students who give in to angry outbursts. If you are unskilled or inexperienced in working with these students, you can easily react in ways that escalate the student's anger and make the situation worse. Examples of actions that might inappropriately escalate student anger are using sarcasm and humiliation, disciplining the student in front of other students, making inappropriate or irrational threats, touching or otherwise making physical contact with the student, raising your voice and trying to outshout the student, or getting too close to the student when dealing with his or her anger.

Let's look at an example of a situation in which the teacher is at fault for aggravating a student who is already angry.

> Drew, a 5th grade boy, is upset and angry after recess because another boy wouldn't let him play basketball. He is visibly upset, yelling out, "Tommy is a real jerk!" in front of the whole class. Drew's teacher responds by saying, "That sure is a mature way of dealing with the situation. Are you sure you're a 5th grader instead of a kindergartener? Maybe I should send you to Mrs. Jones's kindergarten class for the rest of the day." As Drew becomes increasingly angry, yelling louder and getting redder in the face, the teacher walks up to him, gets within two feet of him, and says, "Now I'm certain that you're in the wrong class and should be in kindergarten." At this point, Drew is totally out of control, calls the teacher unmentionable names, knocks over his desk, and goes running out of the room and out of the building.

Because the teacher reacted to Drew inappropriately, his negative behaviors escalated from inappropriate yelling to insubordination, physical outbursts, and leaving the campus without permission. Both teacher and student lose in this case.

There are ways to de-escalate student anger. Teachers should try to be as private as possible when dealing with the student and give the student time and possibly a place to cool down. They can also make statements like, "I know this is a difficult time for you right now. Hang in there, and you'll get through this," or "I understand how you feel. I'd be upset, too," or "Do you need to be alone for awhile?" All of these approaches can help to defuse a student's emotions without further disrupting the class.

Let's revisit the example given earlier, but this time the teacher will employ more appropriate and effective strategies.

> Drew, a 5th grade boy, is upset and angry after recess because another boy wouldn't let him play basketball. He is visibly upset, yelling out, "Tommy is a real jerk!" in front of the whole class. Drew's teacher quietly walks up to him and speaks in a calm voice that is intended only for Drew to hear.

"I know you're upset right now," the teacher tells him, "and I don't blame you for being angry and hurt. I would be upset, too. Why don't you go to the quiet corner for a few minutes until you calm down, and we can talk about this later."

In this scenario, the teacher has validated Drew's anger and shown empathy for how he feels. The response was kept as private as possible. Because the teacher knew from past experience that Drew had anger problems, a quiet area of the room for him to go to when he becomes upset had already been identified. The fact that the teacher let Drew know he'd be able to talk to the teacher later let him know his feelings would not be ignored, and it also communicated to him that there may be a consequence for his inappropriate behavior. The fact that the teacher put a space in time between his outburst and the consequence he earned for the misbehaviors gave Drew time to cool down. This decreased the chance that he would become angrier and make more poor choices.

Consequences for Inappropriate Student Anger

When you fail to provide a student with a consequence for inappropriate displays of anger, you are inadvertently communicating the message that this type of behavior is acceptable and will be tolerated. This message undermines your overall goal of teaching students that managing anger is a critical life skill that they must master. They need to know that even though you may empathize with their feelings, angry outbursts will result in a consequence, just like other inappropriate behaviors do.

When a student breaks a rule and reacts with inappropriate displays of anger (e.g., threats, profanities, verbal abuse), both the rule violation and the inappropriate anger should have an impact on the consequence the student receives. Some teachers will ignore the inappropriate anger for one of two reasons. Sometimes they empathize with the student so much that, in an attempt to be caring and understanding, they ignore the angry outburst and simply focus on the initial inappropriate behavior. A second reason teachers may ignore the angry outburst is that they are afraid that the student's anger will escalate and become worse. In either case, it is detrimental to students to ignore either the initial inappropriate behavior or the angry outburst, as they fail to learn important life lessons about following rules and controlling their anger. See Figure 16.1 for an illustration of the chain of appropriate interactions between the teacher and the angry student.

FIGURE 16.1

TEACHER RESPONSE TO ANGRY OUTBURST

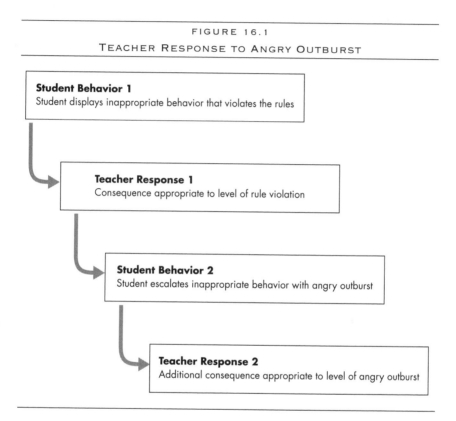

Student Behavior 1
Student displays inappropriate behavior that violates the rules

Teacher Response 1
Consequence appropriate to level of rule violation

Student Behavior 2
Student escalates inappropriate behavior with angry outburst

Teacher Response 2
Additional consequence appropriate to level of angry outburst

Let's imagine that Tommy throws something in the classroom and you let him know that he broke a classroom rule and will receive recess detention. As you calmly give him his consequence, he yells, makes threats, and defiantly declares he will not stay in for recess. At this point, it is appropriate to increase the consequence by giving Tommy more than the recess detention, because he has escalated his misbehavior to insubordination and defiance, which results in an office referral and stronger consequences from the principal. The point is that when you calmly and reasonably deal with a rule violation and the student escalates the unacceptable behavior with an angry outburst, additional consequences for the angry outburst are appropriate and contribute to the goal of teaching students that inappropriately expressed anger will result in stronger consequences.

Some students have angry outbursts on a regular basis and are especially difficult to deal with because they continually defy authority. The next chapter addresses ways to deal with these students.

17

Students with Oppositional Defiant Disorder

Students who have been diagnosed with oppositional defiant disorder (ODD) can pose extreme challenges to teachers and other building staff. Throughout the years, these students have been given various labels, such as explosive personality disorder, behavior disorder, adaptive behavior disorder, and antisocial disorder (Hall & Hall, 2003). Some of the common behavior patterns these students display in and out of the classroom include frequent aggression, temper tantrums, failure to respect others' property, defiance, refusal to comply with instructions, violent behaviors, and repeated displays of resentment.

It is important for staff members to be careful with the term ODD, as there is sometimes a tendency to refer to a student as having ODD if he or she exhibits some aggressive or destructive behaviors. Staff members must remember that for a student to be diagnosed as having ODD, that student must have had an official assessment that involves a team of professionals (Hall & Hall, 2003).

In this chapter, you will learn some characteristics and factors related to ODD, strategies that should be avoided when working with students with ODD, and techniques that can help the students improve and better control their behaviors.

ODD Factors

There are several factors that can increase the likelihood or severity of ODD. These include family stress, poor parenting skills, genetic factors, and watching numerous acts of violence and crime on television (Staub,

1996). Hall and Hall (2003) list temperament, parental stress, and parents with marginal disciplining and nurturing skills as the three main factors that put children at risk for ODD. According to the Halls, some children are hard to parent due to inherent temperament—they throw tantrums and can become inconsolable at a young age. Parents with poor parenting skills reinforce noncompliance by withdrawing requests when their children become defiant. Parental stress can be triggered either by external forces (single parenting, poor parenting skills) or internal ones (depression or some other mood disorder). If all three of the Halls' factors are present, it is almost inevitable that a child will develop ODD. Once this happens, the child's response to failure is often one of aggression; the pattern is set for a future of failure unless the child is dealt with in ways that decrease the negative behaviors and increase the positive ones.

Misconceptions Regarding ODD

There are a number of myths and misconceptions regarding ODD and how to deal with it. Following is a review of some of these misconceptions and the realities concerning them (Hall & Hall, 2003).

Ignoring the behavior of a student with ODD will extinguish the behavior. Reality: The behavior of students with ODD is driven by impulses, so ignoring the behavior will not have any effect. Also, students with ODD don't even notice that they're being ignored, so they are immune to that response.

Harsh punishments improve the behavior of students with ODD. Reality: Punishments mean little to the student with ODD and do little to change the impulse-driven behavior of the student.

Students with ODD will modify their behaviors in order to attain long-term rewards and goals. Reality: The student with ODD may work for short-term rewards, but long-term rewards are often unattainable for them due to their impulsive behavior. They are victims of their own emotions. This interferes with long-term goals set to earn rewards.

Idle time helps students with ODD improve their behavior. Reality: These students are better behaved when they can be active and task-oriented.

Surprises and sudden changes inspire and motivate students with ODD. Reality: Students with ODD need structure, order, and consistency in their lives.

Threats of severe punishment will intimidate students with ODD. Reality: Threats of punishment only create more defiance in these students.

Stimulating and exciting classrooms inspire students with ODD. Reality: Students with ODD often struggle with overstimulation and clutter.

Praise is a powerful motivator for students with ODD. Reality: Students with ODD often perceive praise as manipulation and control and may react negatively to it.

Strategies for Working with Students with ODD

As difficult as students with ODD are to have in the classroom, there are in fact specific strategies that have been identified as being successful in working with them to improve their behavior and help them be successful in school (Hall & Hall, 2003). As you consider these approaches, however, remember the earlier cautions that one size does not fit all and that some strategies work better than others with specific students.

Redirect the Student's Behavior

When correcting a student with ODD, attempt to redirect her behavior rather than order her to stop what she's doing. For example, rather than saying "Sit down now!" when she is out of her seat, ask her to look at the schedule and find out what she should be doing at that moment.

Ask Questions That Provide Acceptable Alternatives

When attempting to encourage a student with ODD to change a certain behavior, ask questions that provide alternative acceptable behaviors. For example, instead of saying, "Johnny, work on your math now," say, "Johnny, would you rather work on your math or your social studies right now?" Any option you offer must be acceptable to you in order to be included in the question.

Help with Time Management

Students with ODD often become frustrated and rebel when they run out of time for completing academic assignments. Therefore, it is helpful to provide them with prompts regarding deadlines and how much time they have left. Examples include putting deadlines on the blackboard, having a class assignment schedule, or using quiet verbal reminders with the student.

Avoid Surprises

Students with ODD often react angrily and rebel when faced with unexpected and sudden changes. The reaction becomes more severe when the change results in the delay of a special event that they have been looking forward to. Unexpected events and sudden changes are part of life and not totally within your control. However, whenever possible, give the student a warning about a change that is about to occur to help her better deal with and prepare for the change. An example is that early in the day, you state to the class, "Yesterday I told you that we were going to have our free time today at one o'clock, but the principal just announced that we are having an emergency assembly at that time, so we'll reschedule our free time for immediately after the assembly."

Watch for Initial Signs That the Student Is Becoming Upset

Usually there are indications that a student with ODD is becoming upset or irritated. Watching for these signs and proactively touching base with the student can sometimes head off a disruption. For example, when a student starts to get upset, you might ask, "Billy, how are you doing? Would you like to be alone for a while in the quiet corner?"

Build Relationships

Often students with ODD have few, if any, positive adult relationships. Welcoming the student each morning, showing a personal interest in her as an individual, caring for her needs, and communicating that you like her are powerful ways to build a relationship that can result in a willingness to please in the student.

Adjust the Academic Schedule

Like all students, those with ODD have certain subjects they enjoy working on more than others and some subjects that easily trigger outbursts. When it is obvious that the student is having a difficult day, you should consider allowing him to work on a subject he enjoys and is successful with. Although this is not suggested as something to do on a regular basis, this approach often helps the student to get through the day without a serious disruption when indications are strong that trouble is brewing.

Meet the Ability Level of the Student

Many students with ODD struggle with academic challenges that their peers can handle with ease. When students with ODD are given assignments that are beyond their ability levels, there is an increased chance that they will become frustrated and disruptive. It is critical not only to understand the academic ability level of your students but also to adjust their assignments accordingly. Work with the special program teachers in diagnosing the students' ability levels and in prescribing appropriate assignments for them.

Have Preset Procedures for Classroom Removal

With most students with ODD, it is inevitable that there will be a time when you need to remove them from the classroom because of an outburst. It is important that every staff member who works with the student participate in a process to determine what behaviors will warrant removal from the classroom and how the process will be followed. The teacher should review the removal plan with the student so that she is clear about which behaviors will result in her being removed from the class and how that will occur. Parents should be involved in making the plan and should be in agreement regarding their part in supporting the plan. Hall & Hall (2003) suggest including the student with ODD in the development of the plan so that she won't feel that once again the adults are in control. In such a situation, the student can help identify at what point she needs to go to a place for a cooling-off period and where that place should be. When, however, it gets to the point that the student has become a danger to others or to property, there needs to be a plan in place that has been communicated to all involved and that will be implemented quickly. Figure 17.1 is an example of a removal plan for a student.

FIGURE 17.1

REMOVAL PLAN

Student: _____

Date: _____

When the student displays behaviors that endanger others or endanger property, the following steps should be followed:

    1. Teacher calls the office.

    2. Office contacts the following trained staff members: _____.

    3. These staff members immediately go to Room _____ and escort the student to the office.

    4. Parents are called. Name and phone number:_____.

    5. Teacher documents the incident.

Another group of students that can be difficult to deal with are those who exhibit behaviors consistent with the diagnosis of attention deficit hyperactivity disorder. We will review strategies for working with these students in the next chapter.

■ ■ ■

18

Students with Attention Deficit Hyperactivity Disorder

Students who display characteristics of attention deficit hyperactivity disorder (ADHD) or have been diagnosed with this disorder present many challenges to their own learning and to school staffs. MacKenzie (1996) states that ADHD affects 3 to 5 percent of the school-age population and crosses all socioeconomic, racial, and cultural groups, affecting more boys than girls. Barkley (1990) says that 3 to 9 percent of the general population meets the criteria for ADHD. Due to this high incidence level, it is extremely important that educators are knowledgeable concerning the disorder and are familiar with approaches that are successful in dealing with these students.

MacKenzie (1996) says that attention deficit disorder (ADD) and ADHD are both described as ADHD in the literature, although ADD doesn't include the hyperactivity symptoms. The behavioral and neurological features of ADHD include problems in attention span, increased activity level, and decreased impulse control. Symptoms include distractibility; difficulty listening and staying on task and focused; difficulty following directions; a tendency to jump among tasks; difficulty keeping track of assignments and materials; and a tendency to be easily frustrated and overwhelmed. Without intervention, students with ADHD can get caught in a cycle of frustration and falling behind, and their behaviors can have a negative impact on their achievement and success in school.

Zametkin and colleagues (1993) state that ADHD is genetic, the result of problems with activity in certain areas of the brain that control impulsivity, arousal, and sensitivity to rewards and punishments. MacKenzie (1996) says that the good news is that the disorder is treatable and that early diagnosis and treatment are the most beneficial to students. Assessment for ADHD involves a battery of medical, psychological, behavioral, and academic tests conducted by a variety of educational and medical professionals. It includes using instruments such as behavioral rating scales, observations, history information, and educational records. The school team does an assessment following a 504 or individualized education plan (IEP) process. The medical assessment is needed to rule out any medical issues that may be contributing to the diagnosis. The treatments are also collaborative, involving a team that combines medical management, classroom accommodations, counseling, and behavior modification by the appropriate professionals (MacKenzie, 1996). In this chapter, we will focus on the classroom and educational strategies.

Behavior management techniques are often not different than those used with other students. It is just that more are needed with students with ADHD. Consequences must be imposed more frequently, and it is more important to have parallel management systems between home and school (MacKenzie, 1996). It is essential to remember to avoid punitive measures and permissive approaches; these result in power struggles that are ineffective, waste time, and damage the relationship between teacher and student.

Another point to remember is that because even some students who aren't labeled as ADHD also exhibit many of the ADHD characteristics, these strategies can help with other students as well (Levin & Shanken-Kaye, 1996). Following are strategies for the education and management of students with ADHD.

Teaching and Management Strategies for Students with ADHD

Selectively Ignore Misbehaviors

It is important for teachers of students with ADHD to "select their battles." If you do not distinguish between behaviors that are significant enough to warrant interventions and those that can be ignored, you may find yourself constantly disciplining the student with ADHD for minor inappropriate behaviors that are often beyond the student's control. If a behavior is not significantly impacting the classroom environment or the student's learning, you might consider ignoring the behavior. This is where meeting with the school's team—its multidisciplinary team (MDT), individualized education plan team, or case study team—is important so that the individuals with training and experience in dealing with these situations can come together and support both student and teacher in determining which approaches to take and which specific behaviors to deal with.

As an example, let's look at Josh, a 3rd grade student who has been diagnosed with ADHD. He has a number of ADHD behaviors, including rocking in his chair, fidgeting, and calling out without raising his hand. The MDT working with Josh's teacher has identified that the major behavior that is disruptive to the classroom is calling out without raising his hand. They work with the teacher to develop a plan to focus on that behavior, giving Josh positive points each time he raises his hand rather than calling out for the teacher's attention.

Redirect with Prearranged Signals and Nonverbal Gestures

Some students with ADHD respond well to nonverbal gestures and reminders. Shrigley (1985) says there is a hierarchy that should be used with all students in dealing with disruptive behaviors, moving from nonverbal intervention to verbal intervention to the implementation of more direct consequences. In addition, Shrigley remarks that nonverbal and verbal interventions are shown to effectively manage 75 percent of classroom disruptions.

MacKenzie (1996) also notes that using a secret signal to get a student's attention or using consistent signals, like saying, "Eyes on me," is effective. In using special nonverbal signals with a student with ADHD, privately meet with the student to remind him that certain signals will be used to redirect his behaviors. This approach can prevent the need to call negative attention to the student. For example, a red card placed on his desk can remind him to raise his hand before answering a question.

Avoid Classroom "Down Time"

Students with ADHD often struggle with breaks in the day when they have nothing to do. An effective strategy is to keep them task-oriented and active at all times. For example, as students enter the classroom in the morning, they should have an assignment to work on immediately, such as a daily assignment shown on the overhead projector.

Provide an Alternative Activity

If you are in tune with the behaviors of the student with ADHD and you notice she is becoming especially restless, you can avoid further problems by giving her a task to do to divert her energy. An example would be to have her erase the chalkboard or take a message to the office. Often this break is just enough to calm the student down and help her to get back to work.

Display Desired Behaviors on Charts and Graphs

Students with ADHD often respond well to charts and graphs that display behaviors that have been targeted as goals (Rief, 1998). These charts and graphs not only serve as reminders to the student of the desired behaviors, but also act as incentives for attainment of the goal.

For example, a chart could be made for tracking when the student works quietly at her desk during independent seat work. Or a chart could be used to check each time the student raises her hand rather than shouting out a response or request. The teacher, another student, or the ADHD student herself can be responsible for making the checks. It is important to chart desired behaviors that are within the student's ability level.

Teach Step-by-Step Behavioral Expectations

Many students with ADHD struggle when faced with a series of behavioral steps and expectations when they transition from one activity to another or when given multistep directions. Make instructions clear, and give them one at a time. Giving directions verbally and in writing will also foster success for the student (MacKenzie, 1996).

Examples of transitions that may be difficult include getting ready for P.E., changing from one subject to the next, or preparing to go to lunch. A strategy that is often successful is to preteach expectations to the student with ADHD before each of these transitions. Sometimes, using another student to work with the student with ADHD is also helpful. Also, prepare the ADHD student by giving him warnings before transitions.

Schedule Breaks and Activities

Many students with ADHD become restless and disruptive after being seated and working on academics for a significant time period. It is advisable to schedule breaks during long academic periods (MacKenzie, 1996).

Also, scheduling P.E. classes, library time, computer sessions, or group discussions between periods of academic study are ways to add movement and variety to break up long sessions of concentration for the student with ADHD, as well as for the rest of the class.

Select a "Buddy" to Help

This has been mentioned in a couple of earlier examples, but it is often helpful to assign a responsible student to be a friend who can quietly help the student with ADHD in certain areas. Examples of ways other students can help include keeping track of appropriate behaviors being charted and modeling how to follow step-by-step directions (MacKenzie, 1996).

Establish a Nonstimulating and Quiet Location

Often students with ADHD benefit from having an opportunity to go to an area of the classroom or building where they will not be distracted by classroom stimuli (Rief, 1998). A study carrel in the back or a corner of the room or a time-out location in the office can be helpful. It is important that these areas are introduced and implemented as helpful strategies for the student rather than as a punishment or consequence for inappropriate behaviors.

Ask the Student to Repeat Directions

Many students with ADHD struggle with directions they are to follow when preparing for an activity, assignment, or transition. Quietly asking them to repeat the directions to the teacher, to a buddy student, or to the class as a way to check for understanding helps students with ADHD remember each step (Rief, 1998).

Allow the Student to Hold Something During Teacher-Led Instruction

Some students with ADHD find themselves better able to focus and stay on task when they are allowed to hold something in their hands, such as a small squeeze ball, during teacher-led discussions (Rief, 1998). If this strategy is put into practice, it is important that it be used with a student who will not take advantage of it. Also, a diplomatic explanation to the rest of the class regarding the exception to the rule of "no objects on the desk" is warranted.

Set Clearly Defined and Marked Classroom Boundaries

Some students with ADHD have a difficult time staying in one location and not going to areas of the room that are off limits. These students will also sometimes get into other students' space. Placing tape around the student's desk to delineate acceptable boundaries can help her remember to stay in a certain area (Rief, 1998). However, consider the age and the issue of embarrassment when using this strategy. Keeping the student's parents informed about the rationale for this strategy is also a good idea.

Encourage Participation in Extracurricular Activities

Many students with ADHD not only enjoy but excel in athletics and other extracurricular activities, such as art, music, and crafts. Extracurricular activities not only provide a great deal of enjoyment for students with ADHD; they also often help them to develop self-esteem. It is important for teachers to assist and encourage students with ADHD to become involved in activities they are interested in and in which they have special skills. Reminding students of registration deadlines, talking to coaches about their skills, and giving them positive reinforcement for their involvement in these activities are strategies to use (Levin & Shanken-Kaye, 1996).

Adjust Homework Expectations

Most students with ADHD struggle with homework. Homework can also create severe challenges and frustration for the student's parents as they attempt to help their child. Teachers should remember that homework that might take an average student 20 minutes to complete often takes the student with ADHD three to four times as long. It is advisable to assign homework that is at the student's ability level and the appropriate length (MacKenzie, 1996). Also, make certain that homework assignments are reviews of material rather than new learning. A good strategy is to have a buddy student that the student with ADHD can check with on the phone regarding homework assignments.

Use Auditory and Visual Cues to Help
Focus Attention and Emphasize Critical Points

When you are conducting teacher-directed instruction, it often helps to use additional cues in order to aid students with ADHD in focusing on critical concepts. Writing with colored chalk, varying your voice level, emphasizing critical points with a laser pointer, and using illustrations often help students with ADHD grasp and remember critical concepts (Rief, 1998).

Consider Letting Students Use Headphones

Allowing students with ADHD to block out noise distractions and auditory stimuli by letting them wear noise-stopping headphones in the classroom is often desirable (Rief, 1998). Appropriate times to use this strategy are during tests and independent seat work activities.

Teach Appropriate "Help Needed" Strategies

Whereas most students become frustrated during independent seat work when they need help or are confused, the concern is more significant for students with ADHD. You should take the time to teach these students acceptable ways to indicate they need help. Using a "help needed" flag on the corner of the desk or displaying an index card with "help" written on it are ways of signaling that a student needs your attention. When a help signal is displayed, you should make every effort to provide the needed assistance as quickly as possible.

Select Assignments at the Correct Level of Difficulty

Students with ADHD often become frustrated and upset when their academic assignments are at a level that is much higher than their ability levels. While this can be a problem for all students, the likelihood of its happening with ADHD students is higher because they typically struggle with work that the average student can handle. Classroom teachers should participate in forming the student's IEP, meet with the special education teacher, and examine tests and achievement patterns closely when monitoring the student's academic performance. They should also not hesitate to modify assignments to meet the student's needs (MacKenzie, 1996).

Place the Student's Desk in a Nondistracting Location

The location of the desk of a student with ADHD can have a critical impact on his academic and behavioral performance. MacKenzie (1996) suggests placing the student's desk near the teacher's desk, with his back to other students. Remember that students with ADHD can easily be distracted when they sit next to windows, mobiles, and artistic displays. They should be in low-traffic areas, such as away from the door, the drinking fountain, and the pencil sharpener. It is desirable to place the desk next to students who are calm and have a history of sitting quietly during teacher-led discussions and independent seat work.

Assign Jobs

Assigning classroom jobs whenever possible to students with ADHD will help build their self-esteem, improve the teacher-student relationship, and diffuse high levels of energy (MacKenzie, 1996). Examples of appropriate jobs include collecting student work, taking messages to the office, taking down students' chairs, and passing out papers. A key time to do this in order to head off further problems is when the student is beginning to become disruptive.

Use Stretch Times

With all students, but especially with students with ADHD, it's a good idea to have stretch breaks embedded within or between long periods of academic study, such as extended discussion periods or long tests.

Use Findings from Time Studies

Time studies indicate that short-term memory peaks at 9:00 a.m. and long-term memory peaks at 3:00 p.m (Armstrong, 1999). You should use this knowledge in planning your daily schedule. Plan to give pop quizzes, lectures, and drills in the morning and focus on motor activities, projects, music, P.E., and art activities in the afternoon.

Build on Incidental Learning Capabilities

Studies indicate that students with ADHD often learn incidental facts that they aren't taught (Armstrong, 1999). For example, they may know how many dots are on the wall or the number of cars in the parking lot. Take advantage of this skill by posting spelling words on the wall before tests or putting math facts on bulletin boards.

19

Bullies

Bullying has been prevalent in schools since the beginning of formalized education. Most educators realize that bullying can have a devastatingly negative impact on student comfort levels, on the building atmosphere, and on student learning. Hoover and Oliver (1996) state that 75 to 90 percent of students report having suffered harassment at the hands of fellow students over their school careers and that 15 percent of students in grades 4 through 8 have been severely distressed by bullying. Studies report that bullies are five times more likely than students who are not bullies to have serious criminal records by the time they are 30 years of age (Hoover & Oliver, 1996). Due to the detrimental effects of bullying on the educational environment, many states are now requiring schools to have antibullying policies in place.

According to Olweus (1993), "a person is being bullied or victimized when he or she is exposed, repeatedly and over time, to negative actions on the part of one or more persons" (p. 413). Hoover and Oliver (1996) describe bullying as psychological or physical harassment by a tormentor. The harassment can include physical, verbal, sexual, or social ostracism. The victim is usually weaker physically or emotionally than the tormentor, and the harassment can result in humiliation or injury.

There are home factors and school factors that contribute to bullying behaviors. Olweus (1993) identifies four parenting practices that can lead to the creation of bullies: the emotional attitude of the parents, a permissive parenting attitude, physical discipline and emotional outbursts by the parents, and the temperament of the child. Other contributors to bullying behaviors include hereditary factors and the amount of violence witnessed on TV, in movies, and in video games. Specific characteristics of typical bullies may include having a need to dominate; being physically stronger than their victims; being hot-tempered, oppositional, and defiant; having a positive view of themselves; showing little empathy towards others; engaging in antisocial behaviors at a young age; developing a negative attitude toward school; and usually having at least a small group of supporters (Olweus, 1993).

There are also certain characteristics that increase the likelihood that a particular child will be a victim of bullying (Olweus, 1993), and some victims may have a combination of these characteristics. They may be physically weaker than their peers and be overly emotional and prone to tears. They may not be involved in sports to a typical extent. They are rarely assertive and have poor self-esteem, making them easy targets. And they usually relate better to adults than their peers.

The attitudes, routines, and behaviors of the school staff in dealing with bullying behaviors can also have an effect on bullying in the school (Olweus, 1993). In other words, there are things that school staffs can do to deal with, and to decrease the level of, bullying behavior in their school. Schools and individual staff members can and should deal with bullies and bullying behavior in order to contribute to a safe and orderly school environment, one free of threat and intimidation. A good place to start is by providing staff inservice training so that teachers and staff have a common philosophy and knowledge base from which to work. In order to determine the collective philosophy of the staff, Beane (1999) suggests that the following statements be discussed to see where there is agreement and where work needs to be done:

• Bullying is not a problem in my classroom or school.
• Bullying is normal, and kids can handle it.
• I was bullied in school, and I survived. These kids will, too.
• Why should I be concerned about bullying? I've got to concentrate on teaching.

Staff members should receive training on the two main ways they can help students who are victims of bullies. The first thing is to provide a safe learning environment. This has been the focus of this entire book, so if you are doing these things, you are addressing the issue of protecting students from bullies. Another important step is to hold classroom discussions on bullying to train students how to deal with bullies. The purpose of class-room bullying awareness discussions is to help students understand what actions constitute bullying, how other students feel about bullying, why bullying hurts a student's popularity, and how to get help.

A good way to begin a classroom discussion about bullying is to say, "Class, today we are going to discuss a topic that is probably very important to each of you. That topic is bullying. Please give me your reactions to each of the following questions." Figure 19.1 has a list of questions you can use to stimulate discussion.

FIGURE 19.1
CLASSROOM BULLYING AWARENESS DISCUSSION

- What is bullying? Why do some kids bully others?
- Have you been bullied? How did it feel? What did you do?
- Are kids who bully others popular? Why or why not?
- How do you feel when you see kids being bullied?
- Would you like to help victims of bullies?
- Do you know what the bullying myths are?

The last question in Figure 19.1 refers to myths associated with bullying that students and even staff members may believe to be true (Beane, 1999). Following is a review of some of these myths and the associated reality of each. These should be taught to staff as well as to students.

Myth: Bullying is only hitting. Reality: Bullying can be much more than hitting. It can be intimidation, harassment, and social ostracism.

Myth: Only babies complain about bullying. Reality: Students are not babies if they complain about bullying. Bullying is cruel and unjustified. Students need to understand that their school should be free from bullying and that they should speak up against bullying.

Myth: Fighting is the best way to stop bullying. Reality: Resorting to violence when dealing with bullying only propagates violence. Also, when students turn to violence to deal with a wrong, it is not always the victim who is the last person standing. It is important to teach students other ways to deal with violence and bullying.

Myth: Bullying teaches kids to be tough. Reality: Bullying does not have a silver lining. It teaches students to fear school, to be nervous, and to be insecure.

Myth: Telling on a bully is "ratting." Reality: Telling on a bully is reporting, not ratting. Reporting is telling on somebody to help that person or someone else; ratting is telling on somebody to get him or her in trouble.

In addition to including information about the myths in the classroom discussions, you should review strategies that students can use when they are bullied. Students often don't think there is anything they can do about bullying other than lash out with violence. Instead, they should be taught the following strategies:

- Relax and consider the options.
- Say "Stop!" and walk away.
- Stand by an adult.
- Bore the bully.
- Use humor.
- Act like you don't notice the bullying.
- Agree with everything the bully says and walk away.
- Tell a teacher.

In your classroom discussions, you should also ask the students what nonviolent approaches have worked for them. Discuss the appropriateness of the different strategies the students share.

Another group that is hurt by bullying is the students who witness the bullying. Witnesses often feel helpless and wish they could intervene. You should also have discussions with your class concerning what they can do when they witness bullying. Include these strategies:

- Don't join in.
- Don't watch.
- Tell the bully to stop.
- Be nice to the victim.
- Encourage the victim to leave with you.
- Get an adult.

Again, you should ask your class what nonviolent approaches they have used effectively when they have witnessed bullying, and discuss the appropriateness of these approaches.

The goal of these classroom discussions is to teach students that there are effective, nonviolent strategies they can use when they are bullied or when they witness bullying and that these strategies are not difficult to put into practice. An extension lesson you can teach involves having students pick one or two strategies that seem to be most appropriate for them and encouraging them to practice using these strategies in a role-play situation.

The final group of students who need help are the bullies themselves. Studies indicate that students who have a history of bullying others often have a serious criminal record by the time they are 30 (Hoover & Oliver, 1996). These students are often very unpopular and have a difficult time at school and in the workplace. It is therefore critical for staff members to do whatever they can to help them change their bullying behavior into more socially acceptable conduct. As we stated earlier, the best way to help both the bully and the students who are bullied is to provide a safe, structured school environment—this is the goal of this entire book. In addition to that, providing the bully with appropriate leadership opportunities sometimes works (Beane, 1999). These students often have very strong leadership potential; the trick is to direct this potential into channels that are appropriate to their skills and their developmental level. Examples of ways to help students be leaders rather than bullies include giving them classroom responsibilities, asking them to lead classroom discussions, and offering them a chance to tutor other students.

Another strategy to use in working with bullies is to develop good relations with them and be a good role model for them. Positive relationships with students and adults are often lacking in a bully's life. We spent time in Chapter 1 talking about ways to develop favorable teacher-student relationships with all students. These same strategies should be used with bullies. The process often takes a more conscious effort when you are working with bullies, as they can have traits that make it difficult to like them. The point is that they need your attention and relationship probably more than do other students in your classroom. As part of the relationship building, you should try to bring attention to the positive aspects of your students through showing off their successes, providing public and private recognition, and communicating positive expectations. Always keep in mind the developmental level of the students and their individual personalities, as some students prefer private to public attention.

Hoover and Oliver (1996) suggest surveying your class to determine the level of bullying that is occurring and also to gauge the effects of your discussions on the amount of bullying behavior that occurs throughout the year. When you are developing a survey, it is important to design it so that it indicates if the bullying is increasing or decreasing. It should also provide information regarding the frequency of the bullying, when the bullying is occurring, where the bullying is occurring, and who is doing the bullying. It should be short, easy to administer, and easy to score. The most effective surveys are the ones that require the students to answer a few questions simply by responding "yes" or "no." Figure 19.2 is an example of a survey for grades 6, 7, and 8 that you can use as a measure to determine the level of bullying in your classroom throughout the year.

FIGURE 19.2

STUDENT BULLYING SURVEY

Sex: M F

1. Have you been physically bullied over the last month (e.g., hit, kicked, punched, pinched, tripped)?
   a. Not at all   b. Once   c. A few times   d. Many times

2. Have you been bullied over the last month in other ways (e.g., teased, intimidated, harassed, humiliated)?
   a. Not at all   b. Once   c. A few times   d. Many times

3. If you were bullied over the last month, do you feel you were able to handle it on your own?
   a. I was not bullied   b. I was bullied, and I handled it on my own   c. I was bullied, but I was not able to handle it on my own

4. If you were bullied over the last month, did you go to an adult for help?
   a. I was not bullied   b. I was bullied, and I did go to an adult for help   c. I was bullied, but I did not go to an adult for help

5. If you were bullied over the last month, by whom were you bullied?
   a. I was not bullied   b. Mostly boys   c. Mostly girls

6. If you were bullied over the last month, what were the ages of the students who bullied you?
   a. I was not bullied   b. Younger students   c. Older students   d. Students my own age

7. If you were bullied over the last month, where did the bullying occur?
   a. I was not bullied   b. In my classroom   c. In the hallways   d. In the lunchroom   e. At the bus stop

8. If you were bullied over the last month, what time of the day did the bullying occur?
   a. I was not bullied   b. Before school   c. During school   d. After school

9. Have you seen other kids being bullied at school?
   a. Yes   b. No

10. Should the teacher talk more to the class about bullying and how kids should handle it?
    a. Yes   b. No

The issue of bullying is an important one that some states are requiring schools to address by law. Even if it is not required, we encourage you to deal proactively with bullying to create a safe learning environment for all students and to improve the climate in your classroom and in the entire building.

End of Section Reflection Questions

1. What new strategies did you learn for dealing with the challenging student?
2. What new strategies will you apply in your classroom with regard to classroom disruptions?
3. What were the most important concepts you learned relating to major rule violations?
4. What were some new things you learned about dealing with anger management issues?
5. What were major concepts you learned about working with students with ODD?
6. What were major concepts you learned about working with students with ADHD?
7. What will you do in your classroom to address whatever bullying issues exist?

Final Thought

The responsibility we all have as educators is immense, and it has far-reaching implications into the life of each child we interact with. Every one of us can think of a wonderful teacher and a not-so-wonderful teacher whom we encountered during our own educational career. Each of these teachers affected us in powerful, yet very different ways. It is up to us to remember to develop powerful and positive relationships with students while at the same time being consistent and firm in our expectations. When we are able to do this on a daily basis, we are helping to develop respectful, honest, and contributing members of society for the future.

Ginott (1972) stated this powerfully and succinctly in his book *Teacher and Child:*

> Dear Teachers:
>
> I am a survivor of a concentration camp. My eyes saw what no person should witness. Gas chambers built by learned engineers. Children poisoned by educated physicians. Infants killed by trained nurses. Women and babies shot and burned by high school and college graduates.
>
> So I am suspicious of education. My request is: help your students become human. Your efforts must never produce learned monsters, skilled psychopaths or educated Eichmanns. Reading, writing and arithmetic are important only if they serve to make our children more humane. (p. 245)

We encourage you to have clear, consistent rules and parameters and fair, meaningful consequences. But above all, be strong role models for your students and form positive, caring relationships. For your efforts, you will be remembered by your students as one of those wonderful teachers who made a positive difference in their lives.

Bibliography

Adelman, H. S., & Taylor, L. (2002). School counselors and school reform: New directions. *Professional School Counseling, 5*(4), 235–248.

Albert, L. (1989). *A teacher's guide to cooperative discipline: How to manage your classroom and promote self-esteem.* Circle Pines, MN: American Guidance Service.

Armstrong, T. (1999). *ADD/ADHD alternatives in the classroom.* Alexandria, VA: Association for Supervision and Curriculum Development.

Barkley, R. A. (1990). *Attention-deficit hyperactivity disorder: A handbook for diagnosis and treatment.* New York: Guilford Press.

Beane, A. L. (1999). *The bully free classroom: Over 100 tips and strategies for teachers K–8.* Minneapolis, MN: Free Spirit Publishing.

Canter, L., & Canter, M. (1997). *Lee Canter's assertive discipline: Positive behavior management for today's classroom.* Santa Monica, CA: Lee Canter and Associates.

Coloroso, B. (1994). *Kids are worth it!: Giving your child the gift of inner discipline.* New York: Avon Books.

Curwin, R. L., & Mendler, A. N. (1988). *Discipline with dignity.* Alexandria, VA: Association for Supervision and Curriculum Development.

Dreikurs, R., Grunwald, B. B., & Peppe, F. C. (1998). *Maintaining sanity in the classroom: Classroom management techniques* (2nd ed.). Washington, DC: Accelerated Development.

French, J., & Raven, B. (1960). The bases for social power. In D. Cartwright & A. Zander (Eds.), *Group dynamics: Research and theory.* New York: Harper and Row.

Ginott, H. (1972). *Teacher and child: A book for parents and teachers.* New York: Macmillan.

Glasser, W. (1998a). *The quality school: Managing students without coercion.* New York: Harper Perennial.

Glasser, W. (1998b). *The quality school teacher: Specific suggestions for teachers who are trying to implement the lead-management ideas of the quality school in their classrooms.* New York: Harper Perennial.

Hall, P., & Hall, N. (2003). *Educating oppositional and defiant children.* Alexandria, VA: Association for Supervision and Curriculum Development.

Hoover, J., & Oliver, R. (1996). *The bullying prevention handbook: A guide for principals, teachers, and counselors.* Bloomington, IN: National Educational Service.

Jones, F. (1987). *Positive classroom discipline.* New York: McGraw-Hill.

Kerman, S., Kimball, T., & Martin, M. (1980). *Teacher expectations and student achievement.* Bloomingdale, IN: Phi Delta Kappa.

Kohn, A. (1996). *Beyond discipline: From compliance to community.* Alexandria, VA: Association for Supervision and Curriculum Development.

Kounin, J. S. (1970). *Discipline and group management in classrooms.* Huntington, NY: R. E. Krieger.

Levin, J., & Shanken-Kaye, J. (1996). *The self-control classroom: Understanding and managing the disruptive behavior of all students including students with ADHD.* Dubuque, IA: Kendall/Hunt Publishing.

MacKenzie, R. J. (1996). *Setting limits in the classroom: How to move beyond the classroom dance of discipline.* Rocklin, CA: Prima Publishing.

Marzano, R. J. (2003). *Classroom management that works: Research-based strategies for every teacher.* Alexandria, VA: Association for Supervision and Curriculum Development.

McEwan, E., & Damer, M. (2000). *Managing unmanageable students: Practical solutions for administrators.* Thousand Oaks, CA: Corwin Press.

Nelsen, J., Lott, L., & Glenn, H. S. (2000). *Positive discipline in the classroom: Developing mutual respect, cooperation, and responsibility in your classroom.* Roseville, CA: Prima Publishing.

Olweus, D. (1993). *Bullying at school: What we know and what we can do.* Oxford, England: Blackwell Publishing.

Rief, S. (1998). *The ADD/ADHD checklist.* Paramus, NJ: Prentice Hall.

Shrigley, R. L. (1985). Curbing student disruption in the classroom: Teachers need intervention skills. *National Association of Secondary School Principals Bulletin, 69*(479), 26–32.

Sprick, R. (1985). *Discipline in the secondary classroom.* West Nyack, NY: The Center for Applied Research in Education.

Staub, E. (1996). Cultural-societal roots of violence: The examples of genocidal violence and of contemporary youth violence in the United States. *American Psychologist, 51*(2), 117–132.

Tauber, R. T. (1999). *Classroom management: Sound theory and effective practice.* Westport, CT: Bergin & Garvey.

Thompson, J. (1998). *Discipline survival kit for the secondary teacher.* West Nyack, NY: The Center for Applied Research in Education.

Walker, H. M., & Walker, J. E. (1991). *Coping with noncompliance in the classroom: A positive approach for teachers.* Austin, TX: Pro-Ed.

Wang, M., Haertel, G., & Walberg, H. (1993, December–1994, January). What helps students learn? *Educational Leadership,* 74–79.

Wong, H., & Wong, R. (1998). *The first days of school: How to be an effective teacher.* Mountainview, CA: Harry K. Wong Publications.

Zametkin, A. J., Liebenauer, L. L., Fitzgerald, G. A., King, A. C., Minkunas, D. V., Herscovitch, P., Yamada, E. M., & Cohen, R. M. (1993). Brain metabolism in teenagers with attention-deficit hyperactivity disorder. *Archives of General Psychiatry, 50*(5), 333–340.

Zehm, S. J., & Kottler, J. A. (1993). *On being a teacher: The human dimension.* Newbury Park, CA: Corwin Press.

Index

academic strategies. *See also* classroom
   management; classroom participation
     for ADHD (attention deficit hyperac-
      tivity disorder) students, 154–160
     auditory and visual cues, 158–159
     for challenging students, 127
     expectations used as, 7–12, 9*f*, 10*f*,
      127
     extracurricular activities, 158
     fast-paced instruction, 127
     free time, using, 110–111, 155–156
     headphones, 159
     for homework, 158
     for ODD (oppositional defiance disor-
      der) students, 149–152
     pride used as motivator, 16–18, 16*f*,
      96
     sponge activities, 110–111, 155–156
ADHD (attention deficit hyperactivity disorder) students, 153–160
anger. *See also* violence
     in parents, 59, 95
     students with management issues,
      142–146, 145*f*
     in teachers when disciplining, 14,
      142
assemblies, 73–76, 74*f*, 75*f*, 76*f*
assessment, discipline system survey,
   49–53, 50–53*f*
behavior standards, for students
     acceptable behavior, 23–33, 98–103,
      101–102*f*
     violent behavior, 86–87, 87*f*
blind spots, 58, 107

buddy system, 157
the building
     blind spots, 58, 107
     hallways, 78–79, 111
     lunchrooms, 77, 78*f*
     portables, 82
     restrooms, 81–82, 82*f*
     rules off school grounds, 58
buildingwide discipline philosophy, 47–48,
   52–53*f*
buildingwide discipline plan, 45–46, 92.
   See also prevention strategies, buildingwide; *specific events*
buildingwide signal, 100, 102*f*
bullies, 161–167, 163*f*, 166*f*
bus loading and unloading, 82–83

caring, demonstrating to students, 12–16,
   13*f*, 15*f*, 18–20, 19*f*, 93, 125–126, 138
the classroom
     blind spots, 107
     headphones in, 159
     layout strategies for ADHD (atten-
      tion deficit hyperactivity disorder)
      students, 154–160
     marking boundaries, 158
     quiet locations, 157
     seating arrangements, 103, 104*f*, 105*f*
     teacher's desk placement, 106
classroom behaviors
     parameters of acceptable, 98–103,
      101–102*f*
     power base, percent of the, 4*f*

About the Authors

Mark Boynton is a retired public school elementary and middle school principal, and he has also been an elementary school teacher and a school counselor. He received his master's degree in education from Seattle University. Mark currently presents discipline workshops for school districts and individual schools at all levels throughout the nation. He also is called on to conduct buildingwide discipline assessments and follow up with inservice training for school staffs.

Christine Boynton is a retired public school educator who has been a speech pathologist, a substitute classroom teacher, a program director, an elementary principal, and finally an assistant superintendent in a district of 17,000 students. Christine received her doctorate in educational leadership from Seattle University. She is currently an educational consultant who works with school districts and individual schools in a number of areas, including discipline assessments, teacher and principal evaluations, policies, and climate issues.

Both Mark and Christine can be reached at mcboynton@aol.com.

Related ASCD Resources
The Educator's Guide to Preventing and Solving Discipline Problems

At the time of publication, the following ASCD resources were available; for the most up-to-date information about ASCD resources, go to www.ascd.org. ASCD stock numbers are noted in parentheses.

Audio

Ensuring a Safe and Orderly School Environment by Elaine Jones (2 CDs, #504106)

Strategies for Anger Management and Conflict Resolution: It's Everybody's Job by Bob Hanson (2 CDs, #504107)

Managing Ethnic Conflict by Suleiman Hamdan (CD, #502260)

Books

Beyond Discipline: From Compliance to Community by Alfie Kohn (#196075)

Bullying and Harassment: A Legal Guide for Educators by Kathleen Conn (#104147)

Connecting Character to Conduct: Helping Students Do the Right Things by Rita Stein, Roberta Richin, Richard Banyon, Francine Banyon, and Marc Stein (#100209)

The Respectful School: How Educators and Students Can Conquer Hate and Harassment by Stephen L. Wessler and William Prebble (#103006)

Talk It Out: Conflict Resolution in the Elementary Classroom by Barbara Porro (#196018)

For more information, visit us on the World Wide Web (http://www.ascd.org), send an e-mail message to member@ascd.org, call the ASCD Service Center (1-800-933-ASCD or 703-578-9600, then press 2), send a fax to 703-575-5400, or write to Information Services, ASCD, 1703 N. Beauregard St., Alexandria, VA 22311-1714 USA.